THE P.
CREW 1943-1944
MEMOIRS OF
WORLD WAR II

MW01608994

THE PLAYBOY CREW 1943-1944 MEMOIRS OF WORLD WAR II

The Men of B-24 Liberator 41-29399

ROBERT F. PIPES

Outskirts Press, Inc.
Denver, Colorado

The opinions expressed in this manuscript are solely the opinions of the author and do not represent the opinions or thoughts of the publisher. The author has represented and warranted full ownership and/or legal right to publish all the materials in this book.

The Playboy Crew 1943-1944 | Memoirs of World War II
The Men of B-24 Liberator 41-29399
All Rights Reserved.
Copyright © 2010 Robert F. Pipes
v2.0

Cover photo © 2010 Keith Hill Studios. All rights reserved – used with permission.

This book may not be reproduced, transmitted, or stored in whole or in part by any means, including graphic, electronic, or mechanical without the express written consent of the publisher except in the case of brief quotations embodied in critical articles and reviews.

Outskirts Press, Inc.
http://www.outskirtspress.com

Paperback ISBN: 978-1-4327-5849-3
Hardback ISBN: 978-1-4327-5851-6

Outskirts Press and the "OP" logo are trademarks belonging to Outskirts Press, Inc.

PRINTED IN THE UNITED STATES OF AMERICA

ACKNOWLEDGEMENT

Grateful acknowledgement is made to Frank Cotner, Melvin Everding, Norman Roth, H.L. Heafner Jr., and Ralph Fiskow for your chapters in this book. Your experiences added a realm of historical significance that was beyond Heafner's and my evasion, and I appreciate your invaluable contributions. I would also like to thank my son, Brian, for his help in revising this book.

Cover art used with the gracious permission of Keith Hill, Keith Hill Studios, UK

www.keithhillstudios.com

DEDICATION

I want to dedicate this book to my wife, Betty, and Lance Stewart for encouraging me to write of my experiences. Also to my children, Robert, Brian, and Melissa and my grandchildren, Daniel Felton Pipes and Molly Sloan Pipes (Robert's children), Steven Ray Breckenridge (Brian's stepson), and Robert Ryan Spencer (Melissa's son).

PREFACE

This is the story of how a young Texan went from the 112th US Cavalry to the 8th Air Force in World War II and lived to return to Texas. The 112th and 124th US Cavalries were the last regiments to work horses as World War II progressed to an all-out land, air, and sea offensive.

This story tells of the birth and death of a B24 Liberator of the 466th bomb group—the life cycle of an aircraft named the *Playboy* from 1943 to 1944.

It includes personal memories of an aircraft crew after being shot down when the 8th Air Force and the Royal Air Force launched one of the largest offensives on Berlin in April of 1944. There are also accounts from the crew of the horror of the prisoner-of-war camps, the "Death Marches," and the narrow escapes and skirmishes when hiding from the Germans in occupied Holland for nearly a year.

Time and time again, death seemed imminent while two of the crew members were in Holland evading German soldiers. This is also the story of the risks the brave Dutch people took to have an active resistance, and some of their losses.

Years later, a downed crew member of the *Playboy* relives the year he spent riding in a train compartment with two German soldiers; suddenly confronting a German Gestapo officer on a lonely country road; hiding in secret compartments and haymows in the country; and aiding the Dutch Underground members in disrupting the enemy forces, all while trying to get to allied lines with the invaluable help of the Dutch Resistance Force.

TABLE OF CONTENTS

1

CAMPFIRE STORIES

The days were long while my wife, Betty, and I were in the wilderness of an Apache Indian reservation in Point of Pines, Arizona, during the summer of 1987. The excitement of killing a bear that raided the camp was a highlight of the two and a half months that I worked as a fuel truck driver for a helicopter company employed by the Bureau of Indian Affairs. Around the camp, the pilots and drivers traded stories to help pass the time.

Betty, near Point of Pines, Arizona.

THE PLAYBOY CREW 1943-1944

My son Brian had previously mentioned to my wife that I had been shot down during World War II and had evaded capture by the Nazis for nearly a year. Betty was so interested that she asked me to tell the story of our bomber crew's ordeal.

Lance Stewart at Apache Indian Reservation firefighters camp.

Lance Stewart was the helicopter pilot at the firefighter camp. He was also impassioned to hear my stories and wanted his teenage son, Jason, to hear of times past. So around the campfire on a summer's night in Arizona, I began to tell them of my military career and the time that I spent in Holland after bailing out of the *Playboy*.

Without the help of the brave and honorable Dutch men and women who helped me, I most likely would not have survived to tell of my experiences. I owe them a great debt of gratitude. My story is as follows:

In the summer of 1939, I became interested in joining the military. The Texas National Guard had the 56th Cavalry Brigade, which consisted of the 112th and 124th Cavalry Regiments. "A" Troop, 112th Cavalry Armory and Reservation, was near my home in Dallas, so I decided that I would join the 112th Cavalry, and enlisted July 1st, 1939. Their motto was "Rarin' to Go" and so was I.

Pipes with best friend, Ted Skinner, at Fort Bliss, Texas

Pipes at Fort Bliss, Texas

CAMPFIRE STORIES

World War II commenced in Europe on September 1st, 1939, with the German Army invading Poland.

The War Department authorized additional field training for National Guard units, five days in the winter of 1939-1940 and an additional week of summer training in 1940.

The 56th Cavalry Brigade was ordered to proceed to Boyce, Louisiana, to participate in a three-week long maneuver to be held in the Kisatchie National Forest, and I was promoted to corporal in a light machine gun platoon.

On November 18th, 1940, the 56th Cavalry Brigade was federalized and all units were transferred to Ft. Bliss, Texas, as regular army bound to fight in World War II. I was promoted to platoon sergeant of the light machine gun squad.

In February of 1941, the 112th US Cavalry was reassigned to Ft. Clark, Texas, replacing the Fifth US Cavalry, which was reassigned to Ft. Bliss with the First Cavalry Division. The 124th Cavalry replaced the 12th US Cavalry at Ft. Brown and Ft. Ringgold, the 12th being reassigned to Ft. Bliss. The 56th Cavalry Brigade went to Ft. McIntosh, replacing the 1st Cavalry Brigade. A little over a year after I left the 112th Cavalry, the regiment was sent to New Caledonia in August of 1942 to patrol the island, as few roads existed.

After another year (May, 1943) the horses were left in the corrals for good and the regiment joined the infantry, going to Woodlark Island; Arawe, New Britain; Aitape, New Guinea; Leyte and Luzon, Philippines; and Honshu, Japan.

Two men in the 112th were awarded the Medal of Honor. They were 2nd Lt. Dale Eldon Christensen and 2nd Lt. W.G. Boyce, Jr.

The 124th Cavalry went to the China, Burma, India theater of operations, earning a name for itself.

In May of 1941, I was discharged from the 112th Cavalry, reenlisted in the Army Air Corps for three years, and was assigned to Brooks Field, San Antonio, Texas. Thus began my Air Corps career, and the World War II stories began to unfold.

This was a time in my life that I had almost forgotten. After Betty heard about the stories told around the camp about my time as a GI behind enemy lines, she insisted I write about them.

I began writing, and after almost a year had passed we decided to take a trip, in June, 1988, to the Netherlands to visit the families who had helped me to avoid capture by the Nazis in 1944 and 1945. The de Bruin family and other Dutch men and women had helped me and other allied airmen evade capture by the German occupation forces. I had kept in touch with the de Bruin family over the years after the war. I saw Arie and Alty de Bruin in 1968, Willem and Toos with his sister Marie in 1978, and Willem, Toos, and their daughter, Alinda, in 1987 in Mississippi when they visited H.L. Heafner, one of the *Playboy* crew members they had helped. After de Bruin went home to Holland, he called and insisted that Betty and I visit. When we arrived in Holland and I saw the people who had helped me I was almost overwhelmed with emotion. Some of the people who had helped me had lost their lives in doing so.

2

THE *PLAYBOY*

The bomber, a Consolidated Aircraft Company B24 H aircraft, serial number 41 29399, was built in Ft. Worth, Texas at the Consolidated bomber plant. The B24 liberator was one of three four-engine, long-range bombers. The B17 *Flying Fortress* was probably the most well known of these. The B29 began production in 1944 and was used to bomb Japan. A B29 named *Enola Gay* was the plane that dropped the atom bomb on Japan on August 6th, 1945, which brought about a quicker end to the war with Japan, thus saving millions of lives on both sides.

The *Playboy* was one of 18,000 liberators built. Manufacture was begun after the war started and ceased before the war ended. Many more Liberators were built than the B17 or B29. The prototype was the XB24, built in December 1939 by Consolidated Aircraft Company, which later became Convair, a division of General Dynamics. The first Liberator to go into active service was the British B24 D.

British Prime Minister Winston Churchill had a Liberator for his personal use, which was customized with seats in the bomb bay area and windows under the wings. These bombers were the first to be able to fly a trans-Atlantic course. The combination of the Liberators and the long-range fighter escorts such as the P47 Thunderbolt, the P38 Lightning, and the P51 Mustang dealt a deadly blow against the German Focke-Wulf 190s, eventually destroying them.

The Liberator was also used by the army and navy in ways that the manufacturer had not foreseen. In addition to being bombers, transports, and submarine patrols, it was also used in reconnaissance; as tankers (the C109) to haul fuel to China; in search and rescue; and personnel carriers. It literally played a role in every flying aspect of the war.

The B24 Liberator evolved into the B32 Dominator, which most successfully served the 8th Air Force Bomber Command in the Pacific Theater.

Our B24 Liberator was named the *Playboy* by the crew, and I drew and painted on the nose of the aircraft a caricature of Donald Duck attired in a tuxedo, complete with top hat, tails, and spats on his webbed feet. He also sported a silver-headed cane tucked under his wing. This

was many years before the *Playboy* magazine and the Playboy clubs were formed. Since the average age of the crew was 22 1/2 years, the name seemed appropriate to us.

The aircraft was armed with ten .50 caliber Browning machine guns, locations as follows:

- An Emerson Electric turret with two guns in the nose of the aircraft,
- a Martin dorsal turret with two guns,
- a Sperry bottom ball turret with two guns,
- a Consolidated tail turret with two guns,
- and two manually operated guns, one on each side mounted in the waist of the fuselage.

The navigator or the bombardier could operate the nose turret. The B24 also had an 8,000-pound bomb capacity.

Clothing, equipment, and weapons were very important to survival. The air temperature while flying over Europe at 22,000 feet would be 40 to 50 degrees below zero. The aircraft had heaters that seldom operated or supplied sufficient heat for comfort, so it was necessary to dress warmly. First, a pair of long woolen underwear was donned, then a woolen olive drab shirt and pants, and a lightweight leather, model A2 jacket made of horse hide. This was topped with a heavy leather, fleece-lined jacket and pants. On the hands, a pair of silk or rayon glove inserts, then a pair of woolen gloves and outer fleece-lined leather gauntlets. On the feet were silk inserts, woolen socks, and heavy fleece-lined flying boots. On the head, a fleece-lined flight helmet with goggles attached (so our eyes wouldn't freeze) and a set of radio earphones installed. An oxygen mask was attached to the flight mask with hooks, topped with a steel flak helmet. Around the neck were two identification tags, a throat-type radio microphone, and a woolen muffler. Over this clothing was a "Mae West" type inflatable life jacket, used in case of ditching in the water.

A quick, attachable parachute harness, which featured a quick-release lever for releasing the parachute and harness upon landing on ground or water after bailing out of the aircraft, was also part of our gear. The parachute was separate from the harness, being attached with hooks and rings when needed.

Some of the crew members wore two-piece armored steel flak jackets over all of their clothing; however, due to the limited space in the upper turret, I was unable to do so.

A .45 caliber semi-automatic pistol was carried in a shoulder holster under the Mae West life jacket, plus a hunting-type sheathed knife. Along with an escape kit, which included a small magnetic compass and maps of Western Europe printed on silk or linen, we carried personal photographs for identification cards that could be used by the Resistance Forces to forge passports. All of this equipment must have weighed about 50 pounds and the wearer looked like something from outer space.

Later we were issued electrically heated flying suits, which included gloves and boot inserts. This reduced the bulkiness and weight somewhat. I was wearing this type on that fateful day we were shot down.

3
THE CREW

2nd Lt. Franklynn V. Cotner, Pilot
Columbus, Ohio
2nd Lt. Edward W. Dwan,* Co-pilot
Benton Harbor, Michigan
2nd Lt. Melvin H. Everding, Navigator
St. Louis, Missouri
2nd Lt. Norman H. Roth, Bombardier
Atlantic City, New Jersey
T/Sgt. Robert F. Pipes, Flight Engineer & Top Turret Gunner
Dallas, Texas
T/Sgt. Charles H. Doring, Radio Operator
Bayonne, New Jersey
S/Sgt. H.L. Heafner, Jr., Left Waist Gunner
Greenwood, Mississippi
S/Sgt. Robert J. Falk,** Right Waist Gunner
New York, New York
S/Sgt. Ralph J. Fiskow, Lower Ball Turret Gunner
Milwaukee, Wisconsin
S/Sgt. Edward L. Mount, Tail Turret Gunner
Columbus, Georgia

THE PLAYBOY CREW 1943-1944

Non-Flying Crew Members
M/Sgt. N.J. "Choochie" Hollier, Crew Chief
Lafayette, Louisiana
S/Sgt. Edward McCarthy, Ordinance
Dallas, Texas

*Lt. Dwan didn't make the final flight of the *Playboy* because we were supposed to be on crew rest and he had gone to Norwich, England and stayed the night there. He didn't get back in time to make the mission, and his substitute was Lt. John B. Stuart, a romantic who couldn't wait to get home to his wife. Hometown: Chicago, Illinois

**S/Sgt. Dan P. Thompson of Memphis, Tennessee, was the original waist gunner, but he was transferred to another crew whose flight engineer had been wounded and was going home. Each flight crew of ten men could only have one flight engineer and one assistant flight engineer, and only one could be a technical sergeant. He was replaced by S/Sgt. Robert J. Falk, who was flying his first mission.

Playboy Crew, Jan. 28th, 1944, Alamogordo, New Mexico.

*Front row kneeling, left to right: Cotner, N.J. "Choochie" Hollier (crew chief)
Dwan, Everding, and Roth.
Back row standing, left to right: Fiskow, Heafner, Doring, Mount, and Pipes.
(Thompson is not shown.)*

THE CREW

The gunner, H.L. Heafner, had known Choochie Hollier prior to military service and recommended him to Lt. Cotner to be our crew chief of the aircraft. Choochie did a fine job of keeping the aircraft maintained and serviced for missions.

Ed McCarthy and I had known each other during high school days at St. Joseph's Academy in Dallas, Texas. So it seemed fitting to have Ed as our ordinance man. He supervised the loading of bombs on the aircraft prior to missions.

The *Playboy* crew members received their specialized training at various Army Air Corps bases scattered around the United States. Fiskow, who was known as "The Hair" because of his magnificent head of black hair, and Thompson, a quiet man, anxious to become lead engineer (which he did), were with me in gunnery school in Harlingen, Texas. Cotner, who had a serious attitude, and Everding were enlisted men together in Florida. We were brought together and placed on the crew at Gowen Field in Boise, Idaho. Everding and Roth were identified by some as a "Mutt and Jeff" team after the comic cartoon, because one was of smaller stature and the other was larger. This reference did not bother them, since as residents of the plane's nose section, the disparity in their physical size made for the better working conditions. From there the crew was transferred to Casper, Wyoming, for further training. We gunners had to maintain our shooting skills by practicing at the skeet range. Heafner, Mount, and I would go and use three or four boxes of shells each. (An expensive thing to do.)

The staff sergeant who was running the gunnery range would call us by name. One day he called for Mount but he mispronounced his name. This was quite an achievement on the gunnery sergeant's part to be able to mispronounce the name "Mount," but he did. He called out "Moot." Well, Mount knew who he meant but didn't answer. After about the fifth time, the gunnery sergeant was getting really angry and asked if anyone with a name close to Moot would answer. Mount stood up and shouted, "The name is Mount, M.O.U.N.T, Edward L., Staff Sergeant, Army Air Corps, serial number fourteen, fourteen, triple zero, five!"

Everyone laughed and soon the story spread throughout the barracks and the base, but it didn't stop there. People in town would see Mount and say, "There's fourteen, fourteen, triple zero, five!" I guess that it was the most famous serial number in the 466th Group.

Incidentally, the serial number can be broken down to tell what area a man was from, if he was enlisted or drafted, and if he was an officer, along with the number he was in the nation. "1" meant he had enlisted; the next number meant the corps area; and the southeast was "4." Mount was the 140,005th to enlist 4th corps area.

Then we were sent to Alamogordo, New Mexico, and there assigned to the 466th Bomb Group for more training. The 466th Bomb Group received 72 new B-24H model aircraft and the crew received their *Playboy*.

The group departed Alamogordo for Herington, Kansas, for modifications to the aircraft (such as armored plates and armored glass) and issue of combat gear. We then flew from Herington to West Palm Beach, Florida; Puerto Rico; Georgetown, British Guiana; Belem, Brazil; Fortaleza, Brazil; Dakar, Senegal, Africa; Marrakech, Morocco, Africa, and Bangor Wales, UK, and then to Attlebridge, England, which was the station of assignment of the 466th Bomb Group. We flew our first mission about a week later, bombing such targets as Biarritz, France (which was a longer flight than to Berlin, Germany).

4

MISSIONS

One day we flew two sorties (missions) to buzz bomb targets on the French coast. Several other missions were flown into the Ruhr Valley, in Germany, which included Hamm, Germany, railway marshalling yards. This particular mission turned out to be a fiasco. Usually take-off time was in the early morning hours, but the mission had been delayed for several hours due to heavy fog over England and it was sometime in the afternoon before the mission started. The target was bombed and on the return flight we were attacked by numerous German fighters. As we neared the French coast the flak guns opened up on us, and as we approached the English coast the British began shooting at us, thinking we were German Luftwaffe planes, because Americans bombed during daylight hours and the RAF at night. The British assumed that all the Americans had returned to their bases and that we must be Germans. Several aircraft were hit and went down because of the British gunners. By now, it was completely dark and the German Luftwaffe night fighters followed the other American planes to airfields, shooting them down as they were coming in on their final approach to land. Other Luftwaffe fighters were strafing (attack by machine gun fire from low-flying aircraft) the airfields, inflicting much damage and heavy casualties.

After we had flown our tenth combat mission we were supposed to be on crew rest the next day, so we all decided to celebrate Ed McCarthy's 22nd or 23rd birthday, on the 28th day of April, 1944. We went to a pub in the village of Weston and proceeded to drink everything the pub owner had in stock. At 10:00 p.m. the pub closed and we had to leave. It was still daylight because it didn't get dark until about eleven. We went outside and proceeded to throw each other into the pub owner's duck pond and chase his ducks and geese all over the pond. He came out and told us to leave or he would call the MPs (military police). We didn't get back to the base until after midnight so we didn't get but a few hours of sleep before we were unexpectedly alerted at 4:00 a.m. to report to briefing for a mission. Needless to say, we weren't in the best condition to be flying, but we had no choice. I hope Ed enjoyed his birthday party as much as we all did.

Lt. Dwan, who really enjoyed life, showed up later in the day and was really surprised that we had gone on a mission. Choochie said that he, Lt. Dwan, and Ed waited until very late that night for us to return from the mission, but of course, we never did.

Our crew had reported to the briefing room that morning and were given our mission flight plan, which was to bomb Friedrichstrasse Railroad Station in Berlin, Germany.

We reported to our aircraft, got to our assigned stations, and took off. Our aircraft formed into squadrons, groups, and divisions. We were the 784th Bombardment Squadron of the 466th Bombardment Group of the 8th Air Force Bomber Command based in Great Britain.

Our plane was loaded with 75 100-pound demolition bombs and we were briefed that there would be heavy flak from German 88 millimeter guns and to expect heavy concentrations of enemy fighter planes.

The 8th Air Force Fighter Command and the Royal Air Force provided fighter cover for the 618 heavy bombers on the mission. We encountered heavy anti-aircraft fire on the way to Berlin. The Germans were firing their "88s" all the way.

Several aircraft were hit and some went down in flames or exploded in midair. As our aircraft neared its target, an 88 knocked out the number two engine, but we were able to maintain airspeed and keep up with the rest of the flight formation. There was some anxiety when the first engine went out, but we were certain we could make it back on

MISSIONS

April 29th, 1944
466th Bomb Group Formation diagram
Mission: Friedrichstrasse Railway Station
2 crews lost, Cotner and Hitchcock

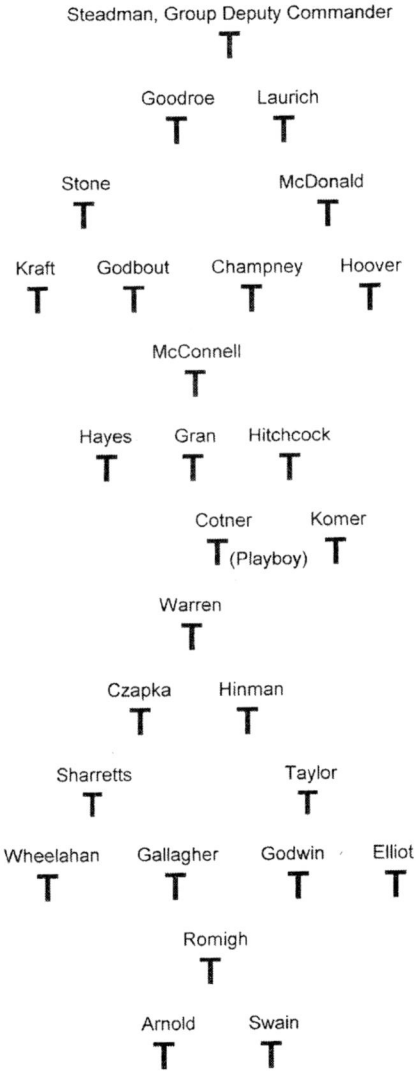

Steadman, Group Deputy Commander
T

Goodroe   Laurich
T   T

Stone   McDonald
T   T

Kraft   Godbout   Champney   Hoover
T   T   T   T

McConnell
T

Hayes   Gran   Hitchcock
T   T   T

Cotner   Komer
T (Playboy)   T

Warren
T

Czapka   Hinman
T   T

Sharretts   Taylor
T   T

Wheelahan   Gallagher   Godwin   Elliot
T   T   T   T

Romigh
T

Arnold   Swain
T   T

three engines. We dropped our bombs on and near the Friedrichstrasse Railroad Station in Berlin and headed back to our base in England, but we were unable to keep up with the group on three engines. We joined a group of B17 Flying Fortresses and flew along with them for a short time, but unable to maintain airspeed, we finally were alone.

Then the Luftwaffe moved in on us with four Focke-Wulf 190 fighters. They began attacking us from six o'clock high and coming in trailing one another. The tail gunner, S/Sgt. Mount, and I were the only gunners who could train our .50 caliber machine guns on them. I saw some of them explode and others trailing smoke as they apparently were hit and were going down.

After nearly 30 minutes of running battle, a group of American P47 Thunderbolts intercepted more FW 190s and shot down several others. During the engagement, however, another engine was shot out of commission. The aircraft, which was riddled with small caliber bullets and 20 millimeter cannon fire, also had many holes by flak from the 88s. The tail turret was knocked out of commission and the armored glass shattered. The tail gunner, S/Sgt. Mount, was severely wounded. A fire erupted in the tail turret at the aft end of the B24, rendering the tail turret useless. The right waist gunner, S/Sgt. Falk, was killed by a shot to the head. He was a replacement gunner, fresh from the United States, flying his very first mission. I received a letter from Falk's family, but I had never seen him until after he was shot and dead. He was already in the plane when the rest of our crew boarded.

The escort flyers stayed with the plane until they ran low on fuel and then they headed for England. We were again on our own, with two engines knocked out and running low on fuel. The pilot decided that the crew would have a better chance as prisoners of war than ditching in the icy English Channel, so he had us bail out over Holland. We knew about where we were. Frank Cotner had asked me to get us into Holland and we landed just five or six kilometers from the German border.

5

DOWNED IN HOLLAND

Heafner, Fiskow, and Mount, the gunners; Doring, the radio operator; Everding, the navigator; Roth, the bombardier; Stuart, the co-pilot; Cotner, the pilot; and I (flight engineer and top turret gunner) jumped at about ten thousand feet. Falk, the dead gunner, was still on board.

Mount and Everding landed in a forest near a castle that belonged to Baron Van Pallandt of Ommen. As many as one hundred airmen and others were aided by the baron or stayed at his estate during a five-year period. (We saw the baron's daughter, Mrs. Adrie De La Porte, on our later visit to Holland, who now lives in a home designed by Frank Lloyd Wright, built in 1938. The baron's castle is now an extension of the University of Cambridge, London, England.)

Mount and Everding were hidden by the baron for several days. He had to surrender the two flyers to the Germans because Mount needed medical attention for his wounds. The Germans suspected the baron was hiding them and he had no alternative but to give them up to the Germans to protect his work of helping other Allied flyers.

Fiskow landed in a tree and his parachute was entangled in the branches. Before he could extricate himself, the Germans captured him. He landed very near a prison camp. Cotner hurt his leg upon landing and was unable to escape the Germans. He was taken to a hospital nearby in the village of Ommen and given medical attention. Roth, Stuart, and Doring were captured by the Germans immediately upon landing. All were prisoners of war until April, 1945. Heafner and I, the two southerners, would evade capture by being hidden from the

Nazis for about a year.

As I descended, I heard an aircraft approaching and feared it was German. I breathed a sigh of relief when I saw that it was an American P47. The plane circled around me until I was very near the ground. He was protecting me from being strafed by German pilots; then he waggled the aircraft's wings as a gesture of good luck and departed.

I landed in a plowed field and was trying to decide which way to go when a man approached me and wanted to know if I was English. I told him that I was an American, and he motioned for me to follow him. I had a tough time keeping up with him, though, because both my flying boots had been pulled from my feet when I bailed out. We were met by his wife and they motioned for me to follow them into a barn. A young boy came on a bicycle and told me to get on behind him. We took off down a country dirt road. I was on the back trying to hold on to a bunched-up parachute with one hand and him with the other. The Dutchman took me to a dense pine forest, hid me in an abandoned rabbit hole, and covered me with pine needles. I peered out a short time later and saw the left waist gunner, Sgt. Heafner, riding behind a man on a bicycle. He was also hidden in a rabbit hole. Heafner and I talked about what we would do. We heard German soldiers talking. They were all around us but they didn't find us because it was getting dark. German search parties were also looking for the other crew members.

Our airplane crash-landed at Daarle, apparently after making a 360-degree turn, in a field, making a fairly good landing with no one at the controls. The autopilot had been turned on prior to the crew bailing out. On its descent, the plane had clipped some tree tops and barely missed a house. It threw off the two outboard engines. Sgt. Falk's body was thrown out of the fuselage. He was buried in a local cemetery and later in the United States. J.H. Kamphuis of Daarle got to the crash site before the Nazis and took a radio from the plane. He still had the radio when we visited Holland in 1988. He also showed us a picture of a German soldier with a cutting torch, cutting the plane into smaller sections for salvage.

The farmer returned to where we had been hiding. He took us to his barn, where we hid in a tunnel in the haymow (loft). He later brought us milk and food. We stayed in the haymow for a day or two without coming out because the Germans were still searching for us.

Finally, the farmer came for us and took us to his house. His wife gave us tea and cookies. Two men dressed in business suits came into the room and said they would help us return to England. They asked us to give up our GI (government issue) wristwatches, .45 caliber automatic pistols, identification tags, and anything that might reveal our identity as Americans, which we did... reluctantly. One of the men was called "Colonel." It seemed to us that they were officials for the Germans, but actually they were part of the Dutch Resistance. We left in the early morning hours in a fancy Mercedes-Benz for Baron Van Pallandt's mansion, where we were given civilian clothing, and we left for the city of Almelo, Holland.

6

HIDING IN THE CITY

We stayed in a secret compartment in a house in Almelo for two or three nights; then we were given identification cards and train tickets to the city of Enschede, Holland. We were escorted to the railroad station by a member of the Resistance Force who was to show us which train to board. German soldiers were numerous in the railway station and in the streets. The Underground agent motioned for us to follow him, and two German soldiers got in between us and the Resistance member. It looked like the soldiers were following our guide. The guide made several detours and we finally eluded the soldiers.

We boarded the train and were assigned a compartment. Two German soldiers in full field equipment and arms entered and were seated opposite us. Trying to act nonchalant, I rolled a cigarette from tobacco and papers given to me by a Resistance member. Immediately after I lit the cigarette, one of the Germans banged his rifle butt on the floor and pointed to the sign that read, "Verboten te Rooken," which I assumed meant "Forbidden to Smoke." Startled, I soon realized that all I had done was light a cigarette and I quickly put it out on the floor. He smiled at me as if to say, "No harm done."

We arrived at a railroad station and a man motioned for us to follow him. A sign at the station read, Enschede, Holland. Until this time I didn't know where we were or where we had been. We followed the guide into a shop, which was a two-story building with living quarters in the back and several bedrooms upstairs.

Mr. and Mrs. Blokzijl.

Blokzijl children

We were introduced to a family of eight, named Blokzijl. who lived there and operated the shop. We stayed with them for two or three weeks. We slept in a secret compartment, but we had freedom of the house until we were warned that Germans were nearby, and then it was back to the compartment. Sometimes I would look through the curtain separating the living quarters from the store and watch the German officers who had come in to make purchases. There were two Blokzijl children I remember, a daughter 14 or 15 years old and a son who was 12 or 13, with whom we played a card game called "Pang," which was similar to the card game Old Maid.

We had been there about three weeks before we could get toothbrushes. We tried to describe to one of the Blokzijl girls what we wanted. She finally understood my Dutch with a Texas accent of "tanden brostel," which meant toothbrush, and brought us a horsehair-bristled, wooden-handled brush that was about ten inches long. As funny as the toothbrushes looked, we were sure glad to have them.

The senior Blokzijl was a very religious man and at mealtimes would say grace, sometimes for long as 30 minutes. Heafner would nudge me as if to say "How much longer?" We would recognize the words "Jesus Christi" every once in a while during the long prayers. We were told that we would stay there until we were contacted by another agent who would take us to the North Sea to catch a submarine back to England and freedom. The man never came.

After about two weeks, USAAF P51 Mustang fighters bombed and strafed a Luftwaffe airfield about four kilometers north of Enschede. Much damage was done to the airfield and aircraft on the ground, and many of the Luftwaffe personnel were killed or wounded. The Blokzijl family's fear of being taken hostage made them decide that we should be moved again.

Heafner and I were getting very impatient to get back to England by this time. We spent the next few days following an agent on bicycles to Hengelo, and then to Almelo. Finally, after some two months of evading, D-Day, June 6th 1944 came, with the Allies coming ashore at Normandy, but it would be many more months before we would be going home.

7

CAMP EISENHOWER

During this time there was much tension among the Resistance Force, and it was decided to move us to a dense forest, with practically no inhabitants, near the Zuider Zee (South Sea). Our means of transportation to get to the forest were; car, horse-drawn cart, canal barge, and bicycle. Once there, we slept in a dugout, living off the land. We were later joined by two other American flyers, Martin Cech of Cleveland, Ohio, and Raymond Swick of Richmond, Indiana. We were also joined by a Jewish rabbi, and a young Dutchman named Jan.

Martin Cech was an evader without an identifiable plane being downed. No one could get any information from him. It was humorously rumored that he had been thrown out of a passing plane during a fight on board because Martin liked to argue…about everything!

We dug a hole about three feet deep and built a sort of sod house to live in. Jan would get milk and bread from a nearby farmer. We caught rabbits and birds in snares and traps for food.

While we were there in those same woods, during our visit in 1988, two women came walking through the area. We thought they were in the wilderness, but evidently the woods were now a beautiful preserve with trails to be enjoyed by the public. It was very strange to be in this place with other people around. There was no sense of danger, only quiet and serenity. Quite different from the last time we were here, hiding from the Germans.

I remember July 31st, 1944, when a B17 that had been shot up pretty badly came over our camp, which we had dubbed "Camp

Eisenhower," and the crew started bailing out. We went to a clearing in the forest and found one of the gunners. We took him to cover. Soon we heard gunfire, so we returned to the clearing. I saw Germans chasing another crew member and motioned for him to come to me. We got back to our camp with the Germans in hot pursuit, evacuated our dugout hurriedly, and got the hell out of there!

We followed a railroad track all night and into early the next morning until some P51s attacked a trainload of German V2 missiles. After the attack we continued on. We came to the station in Marienberg, a small village in the country. We split up again. The two B17 gunners, Harold L. Chapman and Stuart Bouly, went with a Resistance leader. The rabbi and Jan went on their own, and Heafner and I stayed with a man named Bannock at the station for several days. We were later separated, with Martin Cech and I going to the home of a Resistance leader whose name was Gebrit Salomons for about three weeks. I stayed at his home again later.

8

THE DE BRUIN FARM

Later we were sent with a member of the Resistance to a farm in the village of Beerzerveld, which was owned by a prominent family named de Bruin. The family father, Mijnheer; his five sons, Marinus, Cornelius, Willem, Arie, and Peter; Marinus' wife, Kina, and his five daughters (two who were away married), and Aly, Fay, and Marie had built a secret compartment in the haymow. We stayed in our hiding spot during the day and came out only at night for exercise.

A month earlier an OSS (Office of Strategic Services) team, trained in sabotage and subversive duty, was taken to the de Bruin farm. It was commanded by a Frenchman whose code name was McBeef. He was formerly a captain in the French Foreign Legion and a mercenary. The men had been trained in England and had parachuted into Holland at night. Their duties were to upset the German transportation and communications systems. They had been hiding in an old shed on the farm by day, doing their subversive work at night. We stayed with them for several weeks, helping to destroy bridges and other strategic locations. Then the Germans scattered us. Later I met other OSS teams, soldiers, and four airmen from other countries.

Jan, a member of the team, had a radio with which he communicated with headquarters in England. (Jan still lives in the area. We were not able to see him because he was on a trip to southern France during our visit in 1988.) He could only transmit for a few minutes because the Germans could use a homing device to find the location of the transmitter. I gave Jan, the radio operator, a list including the names, rank, and serial numbers of our group of six Americans and instructed him to transmit the information to USAAF Headquarters in London, which he did. To our amazement, the reply the next night was for us to report back to our units in England!

Jan must have transmitted too long because the Germans came that night to attack us. All escaped the raid, but McBeef was shot through his hand and another was shot in the shoulder. The de Bruin family located a doctor and the wounded were treated. McBeef and the wounded man were then brought to the munitions bunker.

The two B17 gunners, Chapman and Bouly, turned up there, as well as an RAF pilot who had been shot down, a Canadian Lancaster pilot and a British Commando captain who had escaped from the Germans after being captured at the Arnhem, Holland, parachute landing in September, 1944. He escaped the Nazis by jumping from a small bathroom window on the train that was taking him and other British paratroopers to a POW camp in Germany. He had been severely wounded at Arnhem and had tumbled down an embankment after jumping from the train. He then was found by the Resistance Force and given medical attention.

There was always a shortage of food, although many good vegetables were raised during the summer. At this time there was now snow on the ground. Suddenly, we saw about 30 or 40 big partridges behind the barn. I could just visualize those birds cooked and steaming on a platter...enough for a feast! The de Bruins told us that those birds were not good for eating. I insisted we try to catch them, so we got a wooden frame and put a net over it. We left a trail of seed to our trap and pulled the string attached to a stick that held up the frame when the birds got under it. We showed the de Bruin girls how to prepare the birds and we ate partridge for several meals.

When I visited Bill de Bruin in 1988 he told about an old sea captain who lived down the road about a half a mile and across the canal from the farm. The captain's house was one or two houses away from the town bar that had catered exclusively to German soldiers. The captain would use his old spyglass telescope. He told Bill that he had seen the Americans who were at his farm and he could tell them how many partridges we had caught that day!

Another time we decided to snare rabbits. We made snares out of wire, like lariats. We spread them across the bridge and we Americans walked across the field to flush the rabbits across the bridge. We left Bill, Arie, and Cornelius de Bruin on the bridge. Finally the rabbits were beginning to get tangled in the snares and we saw Cornelius, being a very practical man, taking off his wooden shoe and bashing the rabbits. These rabbits were called "hassen" and were as big as jackrabbits, but round and fat like a hare. We had to persuade the de Bruins not to hang the rabbits in the cellar to age, undressed and still with entrails. We cleaned and cooked them immediately.

9

RENDEZVOUS WITH THE GESTAPO

When I was shot down, I had all the confidence in the world that within six weeks I would be back in England flying missions again. We frequently had briefings from people who had bailed out and had made it back. The Underground had a very good system set up. They used submarines, boats, and sometimes flew people out. Some would walk all the way to France and Spain, some into Denmark. We had maps printed on linen, a compass, and candy bars; this was part of our escape kit.

Now, after all this time, I had become discouraged and decided to take off on my own, hoping to reach the Allied line. I picked a bad time to try it as there was snow on the ground. But with a bottle of water and two sandwiches, I began crossing the fields to evade the Germans. I came to a road and decided to travel it for a while, because it was much easier and faster traveling. I hadn't gone very far when I encountered a German Gestapo officer and a woman riding in a fancy horse-drawn buggy. He immediately drew a pistol from his holster and ordered me to halt. About this time I decided I had made a big mistake in leaving the farm. The German asked me a number of questions, but I remained silent. (We had been instructed to remain silent if confronted by the enemy, hoping that they would think we were deaf and dumb.) I had no idea what he was saying. Finally, the woman said something to the German officer and he motioned for me to proceed down the road. I walked on until I thought I was out of their sight, where I crossed a field to a farmhouse. Weak with relief from feeling that any minute the German might change his mind and shoot, I hid in a shed until dark. When the farmer came out of his house I called to him and he took me inside. He fed me and put me into a secret room. It seemed that every house had secret rooms or compartments. This room's entrance was through a closet like the family of Anne Frank's hidden compartment in Rotterdam.

The farmer, Gebrit Salomons, was afraid to keep me. The Germans were actively trying to catch him in some subversive work. I later learned that Salomons had been captured and shot to death. I was told that the Germans took two hundred hostages before a firing squad and shot them, actually murdering them. We saw the memorial where 117 Resistance Force members were shot and killed. The place is named Woeste Houeve, which means West Haven. Salomons and Klaus Huibers were killed there, and Klaus Huibers' body was moved after the war to a small Catholic cemetery near the de Bruin farm. (I visited his grave site later, in 1988. We also saw Nete, Gebrit's widow, in Hardenberg during our return visit. She was very strong to remember those times that had caused her husband's death.)

I was contacted by another agent, who said that things looked grave for the Allies. During this winter of 1944, December 12th to be exact, the last German Panzer attack had broken through the lines in Ardennes in Belgium (the Battle of the Bulge), thereby threatening to capture the port of Antwerp, only a few kilometers away. (In 1988 we visited the Airborne Museum near Arnhem, where the British Airborne Division was annihilated by Nazi Panzers in 1944.)

I abandoned my plans to reach the Allies at that time. I had been on the run for about ten months. The agent who Salomons had contacted wanted to know how long I had been in Holland and where I had been hiding. I was reluctant to tell him about the de Bruins because I thought that he could be a German agent. I finally told him and was taken back to the de Bruin farm. I had been gone about a week and had only travelled about ten kilometers, or a little more than six miles.

10

THE DE BRUIN FARM RAID

About this time, Martin Cech decided that he would go out on his own and try to get to Enschede. He made it to Belgium and the Underground picked him up. They had extensive records of all downed planes and could not verify Martin's origin (no identifiable plane). He was suspected of being a German spy and there was no proof that he wasn't! Finally someone thought to check his underwear, which turned out to be GI underwear stenciled with his serial number. He was saved from a possible firing squad. Martin returned to the de Bruin farm after being gone for about a week.

Years later, around 1949, I saw Martin in the train station in Cleveland, Ohio. He was an MP and later had a junkyard in California, near Los Angeles.

One day, while at the de Bruin farm, Martin and I decided to make some liquor to drink. We asked de Bruin for something like corn or oats for mash. He brought us some rye. We made a bin for the rye with a water tank for the water to drip onto the rye to begin fermentation. Our "distillery" consisted of black rubber hoses and we built the fire from peat. It aged from the spout to the glass, and I took one sip and tasted only the rubber hose. I wanted no more, but Martin added a bottle of beer for flavor and drank it all. It was a good thing that we had no more than a quart, because Martin had all of the hangover he could handle for the next two or three days.

Soon afterward the English parachuted arms and ammunition, including pistols, explosives, machine guns, bazookas, and food. These were dropped in a field near our former Camp Eisenhower in the forest, and a Resistance group under the leadership of Marinus de Bruin received the equipment.

British Air Drop Memorial near our "Camp Eisenhower."

While un-packaging the items from the air drop, Cornelius shot himself in the hand accidently with a nine millimeter pistol, unaware that the pistol was loaded. There wasn't any way we could treat his hand because we had no medical supplies, so he wrapped his hand with a piece of cloth and continued his chores about the farm. The wound eventually healed with no complications.

Bill and Arie owned a stripped-down Model A Ford during the war but couldn't get gasoline for it. P51 Mustangs carried auxiliary fuel tanks and when fuel was gone, or if they were going to engage in a fight, the tanks would be dropped from the aircraft. Bill and Arie would salvage the fuel tanks. There would always be a few gallons left in them. When they heard whistling noises and thought it was a bomb, I knew what it was. When they found the tanks they used buckets to recover the fuel.

They got the gas into the Model A and began driving on the road in front of their house. They had many a nice drive to nowhere and back. This was the first gasoline they'd had in about five years.

Arie de Bruin was fascinated with a piece of instantaneous blasting fuse that we had received from the British air drop, and while fooling around with it, the fuse exploded, making a very large noise. Apparently, no one had heard the explosion, even though the enemy was close, within a quarter of a mile. But our luck didn't hold out.

We had just received some guns and ammunition in a night drop from B24s. We didn't get the equipment any too soon because a few nights later the German SS troops surrounded the farmhouse and began shooting into the house and attached barn. It had been a routine day, and at about 10:00 p.m., Heafner and I went to the "room" in the top of the haymow between the bales of hay. The barn was attached to the back of the house with two large doors at the end. The barn was higher and wider than the house, about 100 feet long and about 70 feet wide. Under the thatched roof was a vent-like shaft that opened through the roof. There was hay stacked to the very top in the haymow.

We had a prearranged signal for trouble. The light inside the barn had been turned out for the night. If the light flashed three times, there was danger. We were alerted and grabbed arms. We heard a noise in the path through the hay that was the vent and saw flashes of light fall into the room. Heafner or Swick put a machine gun into the shaft opening and fired. A nine millimeter German Lugar fell out of the shaft and onto the floor.

I picked up the gun and headed down from the haymow because the Germans had heard the gunfire. I later learned that the man in the shaft who was shot had died the next day in a hospital.

The Germans were at each corner of the barn. We ran the de Bruins' two Belgian draft horses out, hoping to cause some confusion. The Germans shot at the horses. Heafner and I threw hand grenades at the men at each corner of the barn through the door and ran out into the darkness.

I don't believe the Germans realized there were so many of us or that we were so well armed. We killed or wounded a number of them and we retreated into the darkness. Heafner and the others jumped onto a boat, but I was too far away and missed it. I swam across the canal and came across another canal, which I also swam. I never saw Heafner in Holland again.

11

THE SMEENCK FARM

I ran all night and spent the next day hiding in a pile of potato vines. I was soaked to the skin after swimming across the two canals. It was the last day of February. I stayed in this field all day and all night. The next morning a farmer came to plow his field. He plowed all day in a circle and I was afraid he was going to "plow" me up too.

As night approached, I went to another farmhouse. I recognized it as the Smeenck farmhouse, a family with whom I had stayed briefly some months earlier: Johan, Yella, Clary, and Greta Smeenck of Kloosterdijk, near Beerzerveld. The Smeenck family grandmother answered the door and I asked for Yella, her grandson. About this time a big German shepherd dog came racing toward the door, but he obeyed Yella and didn't attack me. Yella whisked me out to their barn, and dry clothes and food were brought to me by his sister, Clary. And then I slept. (I was able to speak to Greta Smeenck Tenny, who now lives in Florida, from Bill de Bruin's home during our visit in 1988. It was good to hear her voice. We also visited Clary Smeenck-Jongkind and her husband, Willem, of Almelo, Holland.)

The next day I was taken to a canal barge where we were joined by the others from the de Bruin farm raid. We had been at the de Bruin farm for about seven months. We went to the huge bunker, where some of the arms were hidden, to sleep, but it wasn't large enough for all of us. So four of us went looking for a haystack to sleep in. Finding our " Haystack Hilton," we started digging a tunnel in it only to find out it was already occupied by several men, with no vacancies.

They turned out to be young Dutchmen hiding from the Germans to keep from being sent away as forced laborers in Germany or other countries.

By this time we had grown in number to a small army. There were six Americans, one Canadian, two Englishmen, and several men of other nationalities. We were getting so numerous that we had to be dispersed while plans were made to retaliate against the Germans for the de Bruin farm raid. The British captain and I were put into a bunker (a hole in the ground lined with bales of hay and covered with sod and potato vines with a small trapdoor). The others were dispersed to other farms and hideouts. We stayed here several days; then someone came for the captain, leaving me alone.

When I was in the bunker after the captain left, I heard machine gun fire and looked out of the slit hole alongside the canal. The Germans had shot the lock off the barn and gone inside. I heard no more gunfire, so I assumed no one else was endangered.

After some time, a curvaceous, feminine leg appeared down on the steps through the entrance. It was Greta Smeenck calling to me, "Robert, come with me on this bicycle, we must move you." I knew I needed to keep up with Greta, but I had trouble because the wooden shoes called "kloopen" kept falling off my feet as I pedaled. I followed Greta north, away from the Allied lines, most of the night.

Klaus Huibers was captured during the de Bruin farm raid. He was a Dutch Underground railroad worker who worked for SHAEF (Supreme Headquarters for Allied Expeditionary Forces). Their plan was to paralyze the movement of trains and interrupt communications. Klaus was in his late fifties. He was later executed by the Nazis along with Gebrit Salomons.

Also captured at the farm raid was Marie de Bruin. She was taken to a prison where she was interrogated and held for several weeks. She was only 18 years of age at the time. She insisted she knew nothing of the subversive work going on at the farm. The Germans finally released her to tend to her father, Mijnheer de Bruin, the family patriarch. He was a semi-invalid and had escaped the attack by crawling into the cellar to hide. He was taken prisoner but was later released because of his bad health.

After the raid on the farm, Marinus de Bruin returned and fired several bazooka rockets into their house so it could not be used by the Germans. Marinus then went into hiding with the other Resistance Force members.

12
THE AMSINK FARM

From there, the braver or less cautious of the group made several forays into towns to kill German soldiers. Finally the Germans increased patrols drastically and we were dispersed into the countryside. Greta Smeenck was working with Jan Kolkman (a Dutch policeman and Resistance member) and he may have told her to take me to the Amsink family farm. I'm sure Kolkman and his new bride, Dini, helped many evaders. He and I became friends. He gave me one of their wedding pictures that was taken in August, 1943. His uniform in the photo was the dress uniform of the Dutch police.

When we visited them in 1988, they had many animals in their care. They were called to accept a little fawn while we were there visiting, which they happily added to their collection of turtles, a fox, parrots, and doves.

This farmer, Jan Hendrik Amsink, had about seven children. (We saw five surviving children and Jan in 1988.) We were in the village of Ane, near Gramsbergen. When I was there as an evader, none of the family could speak English. After being in Holland for almost a year I had picked up some Dutch so we got along well. I helped them with the farm chores, milking cows, feeding chickens, pigs, and other livestock, and sorting potatoes. During my stay here I heard shrill noises that sounded like bombs, but were somehow a different sound. After I was liberated I learned that the shrill sounds were probably from German V2 missiles soaring overhead.

Greta Smeenck later returned with a Belgian in his late twenties named Jean Estis. He was from the south of Belgium. He would go into the nearby towns to kill Germans who might be standing sentry or if he would find them out alone. He was a sergeant on anti-aircraft at Liege, Belgium. The Germans had captured him in May, 1940, and he had been a prisoner of war in Hamburg, Germany, all that time. About five years after his capture he was freed when the British bombed the prison. The gates were destroyed, allowing him and others to escape. He walked across Germany into Holland.

He could speak seven languages fluently and at last I had someone to converse with in English. He would come and go from the farm and was sometimes gone for two or three days. He looked like the actor Montgomery Clift, quite handsome. He hated Germans and asked me to go along one evening. I followed him into the night. At one point he told me to wait for him. I visualized that he was killing Germans by slitting their throats as I waited for him in the dark. I wondered what the heck I was doing there. The next night I declined his invitation. I didn't want him to think that I was afraid, but I was just not cut out to be a killer commando.

During one night shortly afterwards, I was awakened by a nudge on my nose. It was the barrel of a pistol, and Jean was saying, "Smell that gunpowder? I killed four Germans and threw them into the canal tonight." He laughed loudly about everything. We never knew what happened to him. I wrote to him at the last address I had, but I never heard from him nor from anyone who has.

13

LIBERATION

Finally, I was rescued by Canadians when they liberated the area. The 2nd Canadian Division came across the Rhine, cut off the Germans, and drove them north to the sea near the German border. I had been living at the Amsink farm for several weeks then. We had gotten word that the Canadians had liberated a nearby small town named De Krim. Wearing blue denim overalls, wooden shoes, and a tam, I was taken by Jan Kolkman, the policeman, to De Krim on a small motorcycle. (Jan remained on the Dutch police force until 1971, when he was 61 years old; then he retired.)

On foot I approached a Canadian soldier guarding a bridge. I told him I was an American and tried to explain how I happened to be attired as a farmer. "You're about the saddest-looking American I've ever seen," the Canadian told me. He turned me over to his commander. They were treating me as a spy because I was out of uniform. They put me into a small cage and told me I would stay there until they sent for an intelligence officer to interrogate me. During my questioning one of the Canadians told me, "If you really are from Texas, you should be able to answer questions about the football teams in the 1938 Rose Bowl." I said that one of them was Southern Methodist University, and one of the men turned to the commander and said, "This guy is not an imposter." After a year of hiding, running, and being scared and hungry most of the time because of strict food rationing, I was finally among Allied Forces.

After that, it was a matter of going from place to place on my trip home. I rode with a Canadian armored scout car for two days. The Canadians had liberated Cognac and Champigny, France, from the Germans. They offered a ride to me and I graciously accepted. I went by jeep to Brussels, Belgium, where I was turned over to a British unit. I was then flown to Paris, France, wearing a Canadian uniform. In Paris, two Canadian MPs stopped me and wanted to know if I was AWOL from the Canadian army because they knew that their 2nd Armored Division was currently in the Netherlands. Finally, in Paris, I was issued an American uniform. I then sent a telegram to my parents saying, "I'm alive and well, be home soon!" My mother had corresponded with Heafner, Doring, and Falk's families while we were missing. No family members knew about our experiences in Holland until sometime in April, 1945.

Next, it was on to Le Havre, France, to a processing center where they loaded me onto a ship to New York. From there, I went by train to Dallas on a 30-day leave and was told that I could get out of the service. I didn't want to get out. I guess they thought that I was crazy, but I had planned to be a career man.

I was 25 years old and married during my year in the Netherlands, and I was listed as missing in action all of that time. My family never presumed that I was dead. They learned by letter that I had been shot down and usually, after a few weeks, the Red Cross confirms that you are a prisoner of war. They had never received any word about me and didn't learn until after World War II was over what had happened to me. They got word on Friday the 13th of April, 1945 that I was all right. A lucky day that they always remembered.

There were times in Holland when I thought I would never see my family again, but I never lost faith that I would escape. Somehow I knew that I would survive over there. Planes were being shot down, planes were flying into each other, but I always felt that I would be okay. Of course, I used to talk to God quite a bit.

There may have been as many as two thousand Allied flyers hidden during the war, and the Dutch people helped us just because we needed help. It didn't matter to them who you were, as long as you weren't a Nazi.

The President
OF THE UNITED STATES OF AMERICA
has directed me to express to

ARIE de BRUIN

the gratitude and appreciation of the American people for gallant service in assisting the escape of Allied soldiers from the enemy

DWIGHT D. EISENHOWER
General of the Army
Commanding General United States Forces European Theater

This certificate is awarded to

Arie de Bruin

as a token of gratitude for and appreciation of the help given to the Sailors, Soldiers and Airmen of the British Commonwealth of Nations, which enabled them to escape from, or evade capture by the enemy.

Air Chief Marshal,
Deputy Supreme Commander,
Allied Expeditionary Force

1939-1945

LIBERATION

If I had it to do over, I would do the same thing. I have no bitterness because I was young and I thought I was just doing my duty.

The war continued in the Pacific, and I was training on the B29 Super Fortress when the war ended in August, 1945.

Many of the people who were connected with the Resistance Movement were given a medal and a certificate signed by Gen. Dwight D. Eisenhower, Commander of SHAEF. Some received a pension for their work aiding Allied Military Personnel, from the British Commonwealth of Nations. In 1945 the United States reimbursed them for their expenses for 13 months of providing refuge to us.

14

AFTER WORLD WAR II

After the war I was stationed at various bases across the United States and Guam. The last three years and eight months of my 20-year career, I flew KC97 fueling tankers for the Strategic Air Command. I flew the same plane in the reserve after my retirement, November 30th, 1960. We had a great bunch of guys in our crew at Lincoln Air Force Base, Nebraska. Capt. Oscar Craighton (pilot), 1st Lt. Woody Heberly (co-pilot), 1st Lt. Orval Gabriel (navigator), M/Sgt. Robert Pipes (flight engineer), A1C Calvin Richards (radio operator), and A1C George "Foots" Kniphel (boom operator). The 98th still holds an annual re-union. It's always good to see the members from our crew and I keep in contact by phone throughout the year with some of the men. In my opinion, we had the best crew in the Strategic Air Command.

I have three children: Robert Frank Pipes, born 2/28/1946, Brian Alan Pipes, born 10/11/1951, and Melissa Lusera Pipes Spencer, born 8/6/1961. I have several grandchildren and they are listed in the dedication of this book.

After my retirement from the military I worked 14 years as an engineer for Solar Turbines in Dallas, Texas. Another employee at Solar Turbines, Doug Hyde, left to form his own company in Durant, Oklahoma. I went to visit him and other former associates and was offered a job with his new company, Universal Parts. Doug Hyde introduced me to his secretary's sister, Betty, who after two and a half years became Mrs. Pipes.

Bob and Betty Pipes, 1993

Betty and I spent two wonderful decades together camping, fishing, travelling, and enjoying our lives and our families… Betty passed away the 9th of October, 2005.

AFTER WORLD WAR II

Status of the *Playboy* Crew
(As of this revision in 2010)

Franklynn V. Cotner	POW	Deceased
Edward W. Dwan	Completed combat tour	Deceased
Charles H. Doring	POW	Deceased
Melvin H. Everding	POW	91 years of age
Ralph J. Fiskow	POW	Deceased
H.L. Heafner	Evader	89 years of age
Robert F. Pipes	Evader	91 years of age
Norman H. Roth	POW	Deceased
John B. Stuart	POW	Unknown, unable to locate
Dan B. Thompson	Completed combat tour	Deceased (accident)

The next five chapters are the memoirs of five additional crew members that were written in 1988 for the original *Playboy Crew* book. At the time of this revision, 2010, three crew members survive: Everding, Heafner, and myself.

15

H.L. HEAFNER JR.

The visits we had with the de Bruin family in 1968 and 1987 were good get-togethers. The last one with Pipes' wife, Betty, was especially good. I'm sorry my wife, Mary, didn't get to attend the last meeting.

Pipes and I were very close during the war, and as I told the people at the gathering in 1987, no one could have been closer without being lovers. We traveled together, slept in the same bed or haystack or clump of wood, ate whatever we could together, experiences you never forget.

I knew Choochie Hollier before I went into the service. His daddy was a mechanic for Greyhound Bus Lines and he was always around motors and machines. He went into the service and became an aircraft mechanic and a good one at that. I think we had the best all-around crew of any. Choochie died as a young man; I don't know the reason.

We had an unlucky day when we were shot down on April 29th, 1944. But then those things happened to many. Falk was the right waist gunner, right next to me, and never knew what hit him. He was shot in the head and died instantly. Mount had his guns shot out of working condition in the tail turret. His back was on fire and I put it out with my hands and gave him an emergency oxygen bottle so he could go to the front of the plane. The plane had many holes in it, from one end to the other, wings and all. Many German Focke-Wulf 190s hit us. Pipes and Doring shot some of them down.

After all these years I don't remember things exactly. It has just been too long. When we bailed out, Pipes and I were close together but away from the rest of our crew, who bailed out either before or after us. All were taken POW's except the two of us and Falk, who was dead. I remember four P47s following us to the ground. From there, a Dutchman first got Pipes and then me and hid us in some woods until late that night. Then we were briefed by members of the Underground. We had to give them our name, rank, and serial number, not knowing at the time if they were members of the Dutch Resistance or bounty hunters, waiting to turn us over to the Germans. It worked out well, as they were good, loyal Dutchmen trying to help us.

Later, after the visit from Arie and Alty in 1968, I received a letter from Holland. A piece of paper fell out of the envelope which looked just like it had my writing on it, and it did. A gentleman named G. Zijlstra had seen an article in the Dutch papers about Arie and Alty's visit to the United States. He had returned the little piece of paper to me on which I had put my name, rank, and serial number about 25 years before.

```
Gaurne zoo spoedig mogelyk opgave van onderstaande gegevens betreffende
geallieerde piloten en vliegend personeel.Een en ander is bestemd voor
doorzending aan de R.A.F.
Name   H. L. HEAFNER  Jr.  34472789  S/S/
Age
Nationality       _AN
Nr of Matriulation(Nr of group squadron)
```

Now it is almost 45 years later. I never answered his letter but maybe I have answered his questions now.

The first night with the Underground, Pipes and I were not sure if the people we were with were going to help us or if they worked for the Germans and were going to turn us over to them. They asked us many questions. We finally decided that even if they were working for the Germans, we would have to give them our name, rank, and serial number, and that was all we would tell them at the time. They were also not sure about us either, as many Germans had infiltrated the Dutch Underground. Thank goodness it all worked out okay. They called England on their Underground radio and verified what we had told them.

We were hidden in a rabbit hole shortly after we bailed out and from there we spent the whole next day, from daylight until dark, hidden in a haystack in a farmer's backyard. From there we met one of the best men I have ever known. He must have been one of the top men in the Underground. We only knew him as "the Colonel." He spoke five languages. He was killed by the Nazis a few weeks before we were liberated.

When we were hidden at the Blokzijl home we were met by two other flyers, Americans Raymond Swick, from near Richmond, Indiana, and Martin Cech, from Cleveland, Ohio. The Dutch said that their contact man, who was to help us escape over the Rhine River and down to France to catch a submarine, had been caught by the Germans, so we had to stay.

After D Day I remember the Blokzijls thought it too dangerous for us to stay in the city of Enschede with them, and we were moved. Finally we ended up at the de Bruin farm in the country.

By this time Cech, Swick, Pipes, and I had two other Americans with us. We had gotten two gunners from a B17 that was shot down in the last part of June, 1944. Their names were Harold L. Chapman of Long Island, New York, and Stuart Bouly from the upper peninsula of Michigan. At that time we were hidden in a planted pine forest. We had to run away from that camp because we thought the Germans were too close, as they were still looking for Chapman and Bouly. Bill de Bruin said that this was later the main dropping ground to parachute guns and ammo to the Underground. The Germans never found it and that forest is still there to this day. It was our Camp Eisenhower.

When the Germans attacked the de Bruin farm we were really surprised. I think it was Swick who actually made the shot into the air shaft, but afterward, all hell broke loose. We were all armed with pistols, Sten guns, (which were automatic hand guns, good for close range fighting), carbines, and hand grenades.

We cut loose with the Sten guns blazing. I think that before it was over they were more afraid of us than we were of them. They were running one way and we were running another. It seems funny now, but it wasn't then. Marie de Bruin was taken prisoner but later released, after three weeks. An old man named Klaus Huibers was also taken prisoner and later shot by the Germans as a hostage.

After this night of February 27th or 28th, 1945, Pipes and I were separated. I did not see him again until Paris. Chapman and I were liberated on April 5th, 1945, by the Canadian Manitoba Dragoons. I think Pipes was liberated a day or so later.

There was much that happened from that night on the last day of February until liberation. Most of that time Chapman, Bouly, Cech, and I were together. Pipes and Swick were with others.

Once while we were hiding on a small farm, Arie de Bruin and a friend named Yo, I can't remember his last name, went out to find us some tobacco to make cigarettes. They were sighted by the Germans. Yo managed to escape and made it back to the farm and told us Arie had been taken prisoner. The Germans told Arie they would kill him unless he led them to where Yo was hiding. Arie was in handcuffs. He figured, and was right, that we could liberate him and keep all of us living instead of him dying.

It worked out that the German soldiers who brought him to us were wounded. I don't know if they were killed. We all escaped with Arie still in handcuffs until late in the night. We found a good Dutchman who sawed the cuffs off with a hacksaw.

From there we could never stay in one place as we were afraid the Germans were too close to catching us. Before we were liberated we were back close to the de Bruin farm. After the Germans had left the farm (they had kept the farm after the raid), some of the family went back in and found many guns and ammo that had been hidden so well that the Germans never found them. Chapman, Cech, Bouly, and I were back near the de Bruin farm for several days before we were liberated. All this time the Dutch were looking out for us so we were able to survive until we were liberated.

We used some of those guns on our last day with the Underground. We were to hold a bridge that the Allies did not want blown up. We were told that only five or six Germans were guarding this bridge. At that time I had a British Bren machine gun (named after the town in Czechoslovakia where the gun was designed and manufactured), and I was to use it to shoot them off the bridge so we could hold it. One of our men in farmer clothes first checked by the bridge to make sure that there were only five or six of them. A good thing for us because when he came back he said there were only five or six on the bridge, but close to six hundred men in the woods. Our little bunch had to forget that bridge. Chapman and I were liberated later that day, April 5th, 1945. We had three German prisoners that the Underground had captured and left with us to guard.

The *Playboy* crew in its day was a real good bunch of guys. Of course, we have all aged a bit and maybe, like I, have added a few extra pounds.

I remember a fight worse than our air battles, worse than helping the Dutch Underground against the Germans. It was the closest that I ever came to being killed. It was a fight in a bar in Bangor, Wales. Pipes pulled me over the bar just before I would have been stabbed in the back. Our officers also remember this fight as we were reprimanded. Now it seems so long ago.

16

RALPH J. FISKOW

As normally happens, years tend to dim memories; however, I will try my best to recall these events. After my capture I was taken to the prison camp for interrogation. This consisted of three hours of "browbeating" plus physical abuse. Following this, the Germans took me to the Ommen city jail, where I spent the night in a five-by-seven-foot cell. The following day the other members of the crew who were captured were brought to the jail and we were all moved by truck to Rotterdam. We spent a couple of days in Rotterdam and then were transferred to Stalag Dolag Luft Oberusel, located in Frankfurt, via Cologne. After some more interrogation and abuse we were split up.

Cotner, Roth, and Everding were sent to Stalag Luft III. Mount, Doring, and I were sent to Stalag Luft VI, located in East Prussia. The town was Keithheine, along the Baltic Sea. We were moved in small boxcars with approximately 40 POWs to a half car. The other half car contained six to eight guards. This trip took approximately one week. Ventilation was nonexistent and we had no toilet facilities, so you can imagine the stench. We spent two months at this camp and were transferred by boat down the Baltic Sea to Stettin. The two-day, 300-mile voyage to Swinemunde was made under the very worst conditions. The hold of the vessel was much too small for this many of us. Again, ventilation was poor and there was a lack of toilet facilities. Drinking water was issued in the sparest amounts. No German rations were issued at all, apparently because the men were given Red Cross rations before leaving camp. Many men could not take these conditions and became hysterical.

One man I personally knew jumped overboard and committed suicide.

Following our disembarkation we were subjected to a march. Our hands were chained and a column was formed. As soon as we started marching, the captain ordered the prisoners to march in double-time. When the *feldwebel* (sergeant) set an irregular pace, the men ran into others in front of them, stumbling and tripping. At this point the guards started using gun butts, bayonets, and dogs to urge the men forward. It was impossible to keep baggage under these conditions. The men lost their meager belongings while they were bitten by dogs, cuffed about, and bayoneted. It was like an obstacle race and we kept to the middle of the road, looking backward while expecting to be beaten by the guards, and looking forward to avoid tripping and falling over baggage and bodies.

Many injuries were incurred, including one man who was temporarily blinded after suffering from a concussion. Smitty, the man I was chained to, and I moved toward the center to avoid more butting and bayonet jabbing when we stumbled. Smitty and I carried a man who became delirious and really out of it. We slung him over the chains between us to prevent him from being bitten by dogs and/or bayoneted. After the war I read an account stating that if any injuries such as bruises or dog bites were treated by the German medical officers, they were merely recorded as frostbite.

When the camp was reached, the prisoners were made to wait in the *vorlager* (advanced camp) for 12 to 30 hours without food. Anyone who had Red Cross provisions when we started was long without them by now.

If the Germans hoped to break our morale or instill fear in us, they failed. We instead felt a deep and sullen hatred for our captors. The first night we had no water, food, or shelter. Soon men began to organize, putting up tents far into the night, and gradually everyone found some sort of shelter. The next day we began to get a limited amount of water and soup, while men who had been able to hold onto their food from the Red Cross parcels shared it with others. Soon we were allowed to move into the main camp.

RALPH J. FISKOW

Inside, the camp conditions were overcrowded and morale was low. Most of the prisoners were underfed and bewildered. Only a portion of the camp was open, and the lager to which we were assigned had twice the men it was equipped to handle. Some men were forced into already crowed barracks, and had to sleep on the eating tables at night. Others crowded into tents that leaked during rains. We developed a taste for ersatz (acorn) coffee and watery cabbage soup.

Air crewmen came here from all over the world, RAF and USAF, also from New Zealand, Canada, South Africa, and Poland, pilots from Lancashire and Yorkshire, tail gunners from Texas, first engineers from Washington, and static chasers from New Jersey.

On Christmas Eve of 1944, in a snowstorm, we were rousted out and began the start of the long march until we were liberated on April 23rd or 24th, 1945. During this march we were starved and frozen, scratched, and suffered disease. We lay in filth, slept in barns or fields, and dodged aerial strafings. For food, we averaged 770 calories a day of German rations. If it had not been for the Red Cross food parcels we received occasionally, many more of us would have died.

We were bombed by our own planes on a day when we were quartered near a fuel depot. I took off into a cemetery and lay between the monuments. What an experience. Mount split away from Doring and me somewhere along the way and I never saw him again. We finally made it through to American lines at Bitterfield in mid April, 1945... Our war was over.

On a vacation trip to Florida, Everding and I stopped in Brantley, Alabama, and met Mount's wife, a lovely person. Talking to her, we found out that Mount had committed suicide in early 1948. Mavis Mount, his wife, said that he was moody and very disturbed about his POW experiences. Ed had three children, very lovely children.

I went through some psychiatric treatment at the VA and it helped me to come to grips with my life.

With kindest regards,
Ralph J. Fiskow

17

MELVIN H. EVERDING

I will try to describe my training and connection with crew number 408 *Playboy*. I enlisted August 7th, 1941, Jefferson Barracks, Missouri. Then I was sent to Chanute Field, Illinois Mechanics School, and after graduation to McDill Field, Florida. I applied for Flight Engineer, was accepted and assigned to the 327th Bombardment Squadron H.

I flew mission training for new pilots, and at the same time submarine patrol and search missions. I met up with Frank Cotner, who was regular army, and we became friends. We both passed cadet exams and the day the group was to leave for Sarasota, Florida, and then overseas, I was sent home on leave and then to California for classification. Frank became a pilot and I became a navigator. Then it was on to Texas for pre-flight and radio training. From there to Buckingham Aerial Gunnery School, Ft. Myers, Florida, and on to Hondo, Texas Navigation School. I met Frank by accident on the flight line just after he had gotten a crew. I almost passed him by. Frank went back to operations and arranged for me to fly with his crew. Then from Gowan Field to Casper, Wyoming, to train as a combat crew. About November, 1943 we went to Alamogordo, New Mexico, under the command of Colonel Bryte. Everything there was a mess—not enough training flights and morale was low. There was a lot of what the police now call "blue flu." The sick bay was kept busy. Many times I heard the group referred to as "Bryte's Bastards." Then one morning Colonel Bryte was gone and replaced by Colonel Pierce. He called a meeting of the group and the gist of his message was "You fly for me and

I'll do for you, or else!" No more drills or playing soldier, just show up for flights. It wasn't long before we passed POM (Preparation for Overseas Movement) instruction.

We flew to Herington Field, Kansas, for final processing and then back to Alamogordo, New Mexico. It was then *Playboy* got its name. I don't remember who suggested "Playboy," but the name seemed to fit as the crew was really a group of fun-loving young men, perhaps a little wild, who got into their share of trouble. Cotner was our stabilizer, although he did get caught up in some of our antics. I never had a brother, but I would be honored to have any of them as a brother. If I had to fly another mission and had the choice of a crew, it would be crew number 408 *Playboy*.

From Alamogordo, New Mexico, our overseas route was as follows:

1. Miami, Florida (Morrison Field)

2. Puerto Rico (Engine trouble. I also had a sore throat. They put me in the hospital. Doctors wanted to remove my tonsils. I told them no, as I did not want to leave my crew. By the time I was released the crew was gone. I received Number One Priority and was assigned navigator on an air transport.)

3. Belem, Brazil

4. Natal, South Africa (Assigned navigator on stripped-down B-24, flying top brass.)

5. Dakar, Senegal, South Africa (Where I caught up with the crew.)

6. Marrakech, Morocco, South Africa (Crew got into a little trouble.)

7. Wales, United Kingdom (Crew got into a little trouble again. They flew us out immediately the next morning.)

8. Attlebridge, England

The original crew flew ten missions and we were to get leave; instead we were called to fly another mission on April 29th, our eleventh. We had a substitute co-pilot, Lt. Stuart, and substitute waist gunner, Sgt. Falk.

All I can add is that when we lost the cover of the last formation and the enemy fighters increased their runs, Cotner called me and told me someone in the waist of the plane was hit and he wanted an ETA as the gas was running low, and Sgt. Pipes was checking it out. I then told Frank there was no chance to reach Attlebridge and if we were lucky we might make the coast. We were fighting very strong northern crosswinds going in and leaving Berlin, which contributed to our gas consumption. I suspect we were losing some fuel overboard also, because of the condition of the plane. I was relieved when Cotner decided we would bail out.

I took my parachute and oxygen mask and went to the waist to see if I could help. Sgt. Falk was dead, killed immediately from a wound to the head. I moved him aside from the ball turret and took his position at the gun. I am sure I managed to get several rounds into three of the enemy fighters, but they disappeared so fast that I could not tell if I did any harm. Sgt. Mount came out of the tail turret and I yelled at him to go back as the fighters were still attacking. He informed me that he was wounded and the guns were out of order. I crawled into the turret and Sgt. Mount was right, I could not fire them. The armor plate glass must have taken a direct hit and the top of the turret was gone. The hydraulic system was shot out. Mount was lucky to be alive. I went back to the waist gun.

It wasn't long before Frank gave the order to bail out. Since Mount was wounded, I told him to jump first and I would follow him by slipping the chute (by pulling on the lines you can direct the parachute). I was able to stay with him and landed about 20 yards away. When landing, I was swinging in the chute and was slammed sideways into the ground, ending up sitting on my right foot with my left leg out to the side. I thought I had broken both knees. I managed to limp to the road to where Mount had landed. He was standing there, chute in hand. He shouted, "Hey, which way to the base?"

"Base, heck," I told him. "We're in Holland, let's get our tails out of here." Those were not my exact words. I changed a couple of them.

We took off into a wooded area and hid. We could hear traffic on the road but could not see anything. When it got dark Mount and I moved out to the road. Within a short time, two elderly men came down the road. We figured if they gave us trouble we could get away. As it happened, it was Baron Van Pallandt and a friend. They were looking for us. They took us to the baron's home, where we met his wife and children. We stayed there several days, possibly a week. The baron was told that the Germans were going to search the cottage, and we were moved out in the dark for a new hiding place. While on the road a Hollander passed us. He saw us before we could slip off to the side. He turned out to be an informer and told the Germans that we had been with the baron. When the baron found out, he had to turn us in or lose his family and his life. Mount and I could have taken off, but we were briefed to do as we were told by the Underground. We were not happy to be turned over. Sgt. Mount's wounds had been cleaned and were not bleeding, nor was the wound in my leg from the flak, and I could limp along pretty well. I'm sure we could have evaded longer if it hadn't been for that informer.

The Germans took us by truck to a jail in Ommen, Holland, and then to a prison. Mount and I were separated. I was sent to a camp in Frankfurt for interrogation. There, I was put into solitary confinement and taken out each day for interrogation. I made them very angry when I continued to give them only my name, rank, and serial number. Since I am of German descent, they wanted to know why I was bombing my own race. After each interrogation I was sent back to solitary with threats of what would happen the following day. I was asked many times if I was scared. The truth is, I was scared stiff. Those Germans knew things about me that I had forgotten. Finally, I was taken to the Frankfurt train station. I would not be here today if it had not been for the protection of the German guards. The German people were angry and shouting after having seen their town and rail station, which were demolished by American and English bombs. I could understand their hostility toward the Allied flyers.

I was put on a train to Sagan and interred at Stalag Luft III. So much has been written about the camps. Anything I'd have to say now only seems repetitious. When the Russians started moving in, the Germans moved us out in the dead of winter on a march that was referred to as "The Death March," where we lost many men and many suffered from frostbite. The old German guards had a rough time too. We were finally put into boxcars to Nuremberg, Stalag XIII D. When I was in Stalag Luft III, there was a prisoner who was a chiropractor. If it hadn't been for his working on my knees, I would have never been able to complete the march. Cotner and Roth made the march as well.

Slalag VIII D was a mess. The straw mattresses were infested with fleas and lice. When more Americans began moving in, the Germans sent us on a march to Moosberg, Stalag VII-A. A lot of us dug into mounds of dirt and found that there were sugar beets below. They were cool, firm, and sweet, but eating them was the worst thing we could have done. We all became sick to our stomachs. "Mooning" was not a fad in those days, but many Germans on the road were mooned, many, many times! For quite a while I could hardly take five steps without dropping my pants. However, we finally reached Moosberg, where we were liberated on April, 29th, 1945, exactly one year after the ill-fated 11th mission of the *Playboy*.

Down went the fences and a lot of us took off. I remember walking through a farmer's field where I saw the biggest pigs I have ever seen. There were two British soldiers who grabbed one by each of its hind legs. A third struck it on the head with a sledgehammer. It took three blows to put it down. The animal seemed to disappear in front of my eyes, as everyone was cutting pieces off for a barbecue.

We took arms wherever we could. I stayed in town a few days and found some food and a shower before they rounded us up, putting us on trucks to the airfield. They flew us to Camp Lucky Strike in Paris. There, we received clean clothes, showers, and food.

Eventually, we boarded the USS *Grant*, a troop transport ship. It was like being on a slow boat to China. First, we went to the Port of Spain, where we were not allowed to leave the ship, and then on to New York. We got a 24-hour pass. Lt. Hall, Lt. Shaw, and myself went to White Plains to visit Sgt. Falk's parents and wife. We could not stay long as we would miss our train home. After I got home I received orders to report to Miami, Florida, with my wife, for a rest. At the last minute, it was changed to San Antonio, Texas, but instructions were to leave my wife at home. There were no facilities for family. While there, I asked to stay in active service. When I had finished navigation school, I applied for pilot's training because at classification I had qualified both as a pilot and a navigator, but they needed navigators, so I had no say in the matter. They told me when I finished my tour as a navigator, I could get pilot training. So I again applied for pilot's training. I was told no, as they had too many pilots. Had they said yes, I probably would have stayed in the service. However, I did stay in the inactive reserve for about 14 years. Then I was asked to become active or resign my commission. Resign I did.

My knees continued to get worse over the years (from the injuries when I parachuted), and after 40 years, I could no longer stand the pain. I now have two stainless steel knees and no more pain. Just a slight scar up the front of each knee.

I would recommend the service for any young man. It's a good clean life, and a place to learn and mature quickly.

The *Playboy* missions, to the best of my recollection, are as follows:

1. March 23rd, 1944 (Big B Engine Factory, Brandenburgische Motor Works)

2. March 27th (Biarritz Airfield and Cadet School)

3. April 5th (Siracourt, France, airfield)

4. April 8th (Brunswick, Germany, factory and airfield)

5. April 9th, (Tutow, Northeast Germany)

6. April 11th (Oschersleben, Germany, aircraft plant)

7. April 18th (Brandenburg, Germany, aircraft assembly plant)

8. April 24th (Leipheim, Germany)

9. April 26th (Paderborn, Germany, target overcast, did not drop bombs)

10. April 28th (Mimoyecques, France, target overcast. On our way back we spotted an airfield at eleven o'clock about five miles off course, bombed it instead of the channel. Big mistake, never saw so much flak.)

11. April 29th (Berlin, Friedrichstrasse Railroad Station)

Playboy took a terrible beating that day. It was about sixty percent plane and about forty percent holes. It is a wonder how it flew as long as it did. The B24 Liberator was a "number one" airplane.

Sincerely,
Mel Everding

18

FRANKLYNN V. COTNER

Most pilots who have experienced major problems in aircraft will tell you that it is usually more than one event that causes ultimate failure. This is true, and there were four such events that brought the *Playboy* down. They were as follows:

1. The loss of number three engine.

2. A flying mistake by our sister group.

3. A missed rendezvous by our fighter cover, which was caused by extreme head winds.

4. The loss of number two engine, and more importantly, damage of an unknown nature to our number one engine.

On April 29, 1944 we were flying a mission to Berlin, Germany. About halfway to the target we received a direct hit from anti-aircraft fire. This hit produced a three-foot hole in our right wing between the fuselage and the number three engine. We were fortunate in that we were able to feather the prop and continue the mission. We dropped our bombs and headed back to England. The damage to our number three engine, as you see, did not prevent us from continuing the mission.

On our return, suddenly the air group on our left began an "essing" maneuver, which was bringing them directly into our formation.

THE PLAYBOY CREW 1943-1944

The pilots of our group, 466th, immediately scattered and began to regroup further to the right. It was during this regrouping that the loss of power by the absence of number three engine had the most impact. Even though we could maintain our position in straight and level flight, we did not have enough power to execute the maneuvers necessary to regroup.

While I was trying to find another formation to tack on to, the enemy hit us. Four Focke-Wulf 190s came at us, from six o'clock, pumping 20-millimeter cannon rounds into our plane. Robert F. Pipes, our engineer who manned the top turret guns, and Sgt. Mount, the tail gunner, were able to destroy two or three enemy fighters. I don't know what damage our other gunners caused. During this firefight, the right waist gunner, Sgt. Falk, flying his first mission, was instantly killed by a shot through his head. Mount, the tail gunner, really took a beating. He suffered wounds and burns and, as I remember, was blown out of his turret and back into the plane. The fighter attack caused other extensive damage, including the knocking out of our number two engine and some damage to our number one engine. The damage to number one caused intermittent surges of power. Had I been able to depend on number one, I could have established a power glide across the English Channel and then made other decisions over England. It was then I trimmed the ship for a straight glide, expecting that it would continue on into the water, and gave the order to abandon ship.

Of the nine crewmen who jumped that afternoon, all of them eventually made it back to the United States, and as of now, 1988, most are still alive, so the decision must have been the right one. (I might mention that after I bailed out, our airplane made a complete 360-degree turn to the left and came a lot closer to me than I wanted.)

Pipes was sent to the rear of the ship to make sure everyone was out. Two of the crew were standing on the catwalk at the rear of the bomb bay, and one of the men could not bring himself to bail out and was helped by Pipes and H.L. Heafner. Heafner followed him out and Pipes came forward to check on me. I was on my way from the flight deck after trimming the aircraft. Pipes bailed out and linked up with

Heafner and they evaded capture for the rest of the war.

When I bailed out I could see there was a hole, approximately three feet in diameter, between our fuselage and our number three engine. There was a similar hole through the bomb bay doors. I could see that the fuselage had sustained thousands of holes and the right rudder was almost destroyed. The left rudder was severed at the middle. This damage was a result of the attacks by the Luftwaffe fighter planes.

I later learned that the *Playboy* had made a soft belly landing at Daarle, Holland, with the body of Sgt. Falk still aboard. Sgt. Mount used Sgt. Falk's parachute because his had been destroyed by enemy fire.

I landed in a little farming community in Holland and was almost instantly surrounded by very friendly Dutch civilians. I had injured my left side in the landing and this made walking very difficult. Some farmers brought a door and laid me on it and carried me into a large house. I was there only a few minutes when one of them spoke to me in English. He said that they could help me to escape, except that I was so badly hurt. Another fellow arrived and came to the center of the group. He looked down at me and said, "Hi, buddy, where are you from?" I told him I was from the United States, to which he replied, "Well, I'm from Chicago myself!" Apparently, like a lot of Americans, he was caught in Holland when war was declared.

The villagers took me to a small hospital at Armelo. I stayed in the hospital overnight. The next morning a little chubby, rosy-cheeked nurse of about 40 somehow informed me in a mixture of English, Dutch, and "gestures" that the Germans would come soon to take me away. She said my injuries were not serious enough to prevent that. However, if it was all right with me, they could take a sledgehammer and break my leg so that I might be left in the hospital longer. I told her that anything would be okay, but before they could get the hammer, the Germans came.

From there I was taken to a very large prison in Amsterdam and put in solitary confinement with two meals a day of sawdust-flavored bread and warm tea. I don't remember how long I was there.

THE PLAYBOY CREW 1943-1944

Next, I was taken to "Frankfurt on the Main," where again I resided in solitary, with the same filthy conditions. Once a day I was interrogated by a German Air Force major. The singular question asked of me was "How many bombs did you carry on your last mission?" This went on for days, while outside my window the Germans were trying to dig up and defuse an eight-thousand-pound, delay action English bomb. I didn't know whether the bomb was live or if it had been placed there for obvious reasons. I finally told the major we carried 50 100-pound bombs on that mission. This seemed to satisfy him and he said I could go and join my friends in another part of the area. (We actually carried 75 bombs.)

This other area was next to a street that hundreds of German officers took on their way to a war college. So each morning, noon, and evening as the officers walked by we would serenade them with a little song. Some of the words were "We will oompah, oompah, right in the Fuhrer's face."

In late 1944, Stuart, Everding, Roth, and I arrived at Sagan Stalag Luft III, This prison camp was about 90 kilometers southeast of Berlin. On or about January 29th, 1945 we began a march from Sagan to Nuremberg. There were quite a few POWs who had previous military experience before they became air crew. I had been in the infantry for three years prior to going in the Air Force. I had a pretty good idea of how to take care of myself in situations like this. Before leaving Sagan I had made a ski mask from a pair of long johns. It covered my head and face, and I cut two eyeholes in it. I was in slightly better condition than some of the others who were inexperienced. After approximately 28 hours of marching, and during a regular rest stop, we found ourselves deep in a forest.

During this stop, there was a horse-drawn wagon, which was filled with German records. These were contained in trunks with heavy metal supports on each corner. One of the horses froze to death in its traces. When the traces were cleared, it alarmed the other horse, which bolted. The metal edges on the boxes being dragged started making a noise like machine gun fire. The Germans thought the Russians were upon them and they started firing their machine guns indiscriminately. We jumped off to the side of the road and lay in ditches for 20 minutes. During that time our body heat melted the snow so that when we continued the march, the clothing on our front was wet.

When we stopped for our five- to ten-minute rest each hour, many of the inexperienced POWs would kneel in the middle of the road and start rocking back and forth on their hands and knees, not knowing they were freezing to death. I and some others did everything we could do to get them back on their feet. We dragged them, kicked them in the fanny, and swore at them. We did anything that would cause a spark and would get them going. Some POWs, exhausted by the day's march, crawled off the road and froze to death.

After a miserable 24- or 36-hour march, we arrived at a town (Dresden or Chemnitz) and were billeted in a pottery plant. It was an opportunity to remove my pack and two packs that I was carrying for other marchers. There I learned my arms and legs had been mildly frostbitten and I began to have pain. From there we went by boxcar to Nuremberg—Stalag Luft VII D. This camp was located very close to railway marshalling yards, and both the RAF and our 8th Air Force flew bomb raids over it. Sometimes our barracks would be moved off the foundations by four or five inches and the next day be moved back again by the concussion of the bomb blasts. The windows were all shattered. The Germans said we could not seek shelter during the raids and kept us inside at gunpoint. We replied, "Up your bucket!", dug trenches outside our barracks with "KLIM" cans (milk spelled backward), and jumped out the broken windows during air raids and into the trenches. We even removed the wooden covers from the windows and used them to shield ourselves from flying debris. We could see all the devastation being wreaked on Nuremberg and more than once said, "Isn't it wonderful that when we get home we'll have the United States, and the German POWs all of this to come back to."

After the end of February to mid March, Red Cross parcels began coming through. Shortly after Easter we were told we would march to Moosberg, which was about 145 kilometers distant. Colonel Alkire and the German *kommandant* reached an agreement that would make the march less demanding on the POWs.

Our officers created a Commando group, and I was selected, along with some others, to march directly behind the senior American officers and the German major in charge. Our job was to save as many POWs as we could if their lives were in danger. We also had some bed sheets to spread out in a field in the letters "P.O.W." or to wave as white flags if the American fighter planes discovered the column.

Finally at Moosberg and Stalag VII-A we found showers and enjoyed our first in two and a half months. Red Cross food parcel delivery was very good. There was much bombing around us again.

Suddenly on April 29th, 1945, rifle and machine gun fire began. As I was sitting peeling potatoes, a bullet went through the tent and missed my head by only a few inches. There was some commotion outside so we tumbled out to see what the problem was. There was a light aircraft flying over the camp. I believe they wanted everyone out of the tents and into slit trenches. As I looked out to the east there was a column of American tanks on a hill, moving to the south. We hit the trenches and the war began again. The tanks started their bombardment and the Germans fired in reply. It lasted into the night.

The next day we were told that some SS troopers had gone into the barracks and told the Wehrmacht soldiers that they should resist to the end. The Wehrmacht were a bunch of middle-aged farmers who did not care one way or the other about the outcome of the war. They made it clear to the SS that they were not going to fight it out to the end. The SS fired a bazooka into the barracks, killing quite a few of the Wehrmacht troops. Then the SS took off when the sound of the American artillery could be heard close by.

General Patton's 14th Armored Division came into our camp, followed by GI trucks and jeeps. The American flag was raised, and I was on the beginning of my trip home.

I was put aboard an Italian liner, the USS *Monticello*, and the minute I hit the gangplank I began to feel seasick. For 12 days I was in a miserable condition. I couldn't eat, I couldn't sit down or stand up. I couldn't lie down. The only relief I got was at night when the barber shop closed. I made a deal with the barber so that I could sleep in his swivel chair. I could tilt the chair in a certain way and get some rest.

I landed at Camp Miles Standish, Massachusetts, where steak, mashed potatoes, pie, milk, anything we wanted was served to us by German POWs. Personally, I couldn't eat anything except potatoes without gravy. The German POWs ate with us, piling up their plates and sitting in their own section of the dining hall. They gobbled down everything as I sat there watching them, while I ate nothing.

Sincerely,
Frank Cotner

19

NORMAN H. ROTH

I find that those of us who were prisoners of war carry our war with us to this very day. We tend not to be very communicative—amongst ourselves, yes, but with those who are outside comparable experiences, no.

Any reference to terrible war years may not be completely accurate. For many of us veterans our war experiences were at the same time the most exciting events of our lives and also the most hair-raising, terrible experiences that we ever had. This is evident in the conversations that I have overheard when visiting our local Veterans Administration outpatient center. When you meet other veterans, literally, one's experiences form a bridge with the strangers you meet.

Think of it, our World War II experiences uprooted us from our homes all over the country and reshaped us from whatever we had formerly been. I was a recent high school graduate.

Ten specialists were formed into a fighting team whose lives, to a great extent, depended on each other. That we functioned as well as we did is a credit not only to our training but to the type of people we were and to those who led us.

From my perspective, I would like to give my opinion on a significant factor that contributed to our being shot down. We flew overseas via the southern route leaving Florida, going to Puerto Rico, British Guiana, Brazil, French West Africa, Morocco, Wales, and lastly, to our home base at Attlebridge, England.

The average time for such a trip was three to four days. We were a little slower. It took us 30 days. I personally enjoyed the trip as I got to see a little something of places that I had never been to before and felt that the war would wait for us until we got there. As a result of this extended trip, if my memory serves me, we were assigned to a rear position in the squadron flight pattern.

I remember thinking that this position was not the best, despite the fact that someone had to be in the rear. The anti-aircraft fire, which is aimed at the front of our formation, with our maneuvering around would likely tend to hit those planes toward the rear. Sooner or later we could find ourselves in "hot water." On reflection, that it happened when it did on an all-out Air Force raid to Berlin is not too surprising. Others on our crew may not agree with me completely. I don't remember our specifically discussing this matter in our POW camp, where Cotner and Stuart (the two pilots), Everding, and I were held.

Holland, April 29, 1944. When word came to me in the nose of our bomber that we were in serious trouble, I quickly pulled myself out of the front turret (my gunnery station), leaving behind the electrically wired soft shoes I had been wearing to keep my feet warm. I grabbed up my GI shoes in one hand, tucked my chest-type parachute under an arm, and made my way back to the bomb bay in my stocking feet. Once there, I opened up the bomb bay doors through which we could exit the plane using our parachutes. The odor of escaping fuel was overpowering. My immediate thought was that this was not a good place to be since it was possible that the leaking fuel could lead to the plane blowing up. When the order came from Cotner (the pilot) to leave, it was with a sense of relief that I bailed out, this despite my never having made a parachute jump before.

I remember seeing one of our little brothers, a United States P47 fighter plane, circling overhead as I drifted downward. A hard landing in my stocking feet resulted in my right leg buckling under me. Two groups of people came at me from different directions across a large field in which I had landed. The first group to reach me were civilians. They explained in English that they could not help me since the other group were German soldiers. I quickly gave the civilian group my "GI Escape Kit," consisting primarily of foreign money, and wrote out the names and address of my parents in the United States. Literally moments later, the soldiers came up to me, took me in charge, and marched me off limping and carrying my parachute to the nearby police station in Ommen, Holland. When I arrived there, I was placed in a cell.

I was the first of our crew to bail out and the first captured. At the police station, I was told by the policemen, again in English, that although my soldier captors wore German uniforms, they actually were Dutch Quislings (German sympathizers). I was assured that as soon as the war was over and Holland was free again, these Quislings "would be taken care of," i.e., killed.

The police were friendly and told me that I would be turned over to the regular German forces, who were to come and pick me up. in the meantime, other members of the crew began arriving at the police station. These included, if my memory is correct, Stuart, the co-pilot, Doring, the radio operator, and Fiskow, the ball turret gunner.

The next day, along with the others, I was taken to a nearby German-occupied airfield and again put in a cell. From there, I was transported to Amsterdam, Holland, and kept in jail for two more days.

Frankfurt, Germany, May 4, 1944. My forced entrance into Germany was via train. I noticed that our old coach car was close to the armored engine pulling the train. It didn't take me long to figure out this location was deliberate. If any plane attempted to shoot up the train's engine, a not unusual practice, in all likelihood I would be right in the midst of the strafing. Fortunately, the trip was uneventful.

The first stop in Germany was Frankfurt, a processing center where I was put into solitary confinement for a couple of days before being interrogated. I offered only my name, rank, and serial number and nothing else. Having heard that Bombardiers were not too popular in Germany, I was not about to broadcast my position as a *terrorfleiger* (terror flyer). The interrogator had a variety of facts about our squadron and group, where we were trained in the United States, where we were based in England, and which city had been our target the day we were forced to abandon our plane, etc. It was apparent that I was being given the "we know all the answers" treatment. After a repetition of my name, rank, and serial number, I was returned to my solitary cell for the day, before being taken out for another train ride.

My chief memory of the "visit" to Frankfurt was not the solitary confinement or interrogation experience, but being in the Frankfurt train station during an air raid. Fortunately, we prisoners of war were on one platform while on another parallel platform, some 15 feet away, were a number of threatening civilians waving their fists at us and screaming imprecations at us at the top of their lungs. While their language was not understood, the impression came through that they did not like us and would like to do grievous harm to our bodies. I was thankful that we were not only a distance away from these furious people, but had armed German soldiers to guard us. Of course, there was always the possibility of being bombed by our own forces. As a Bombardier, I realized that one's bombing accuracy in the midst of an air raid sometimes goes awry.

Sagan, Germany, May 9, 1944 Stalag Luft III. Stalag Luft III (meaning Camp Air III) was my captive home away from base for the next nine months. This camp at Sagan (today located in Poland) was then in Germany's lower Silesia about one hundred miles southeast of Berlin. It housed some ten thousand American and Royal Air Force officers together with support enlisted personnel since officers were not supposed to work under the terms of the Geneva Convention. This international guide was followed by the Germans only when it was convenient and beneficial. This was the largest officers' camp in Germany.

As I arrived at Stalag Luft III, I remember walking, under guard, past a prominent memorial marker in front of the camp. Subsequently I learned that during Napoleon's winter retreat from Russia, back in 1812, one of his officers had died and was buried at that location and a memorial erected.

The sight of barbed-wire fences with 15-foot-high guard towers spaced at intervals presented an ominous sight. I had never in my 20 years on this earth been forcefully penned up, and it didn't take much imagination to know that I wouldn't like it there. Time was to prove that I was right.

Along with Everding (navigator) and Stuart (co-pilot) I set up my quarters in a room designed to house about ten men with some comfort. However, due to the continuous influx of *kriegies*, a contraction of the German word *kriegsgefangenen*, meaning prisoners of war, we ended up with five triple-decker bunks accommodating 15 men. Such close conditions made living there the "pits." There was a lack of cleaning materials and an abundance of lice and fleas infesting the bedding at all times. The wood shavings mattresses resting on widely spaced, thin wood slats, the scarcity of pressed coal for cooking and rations of hot water, unheated barracks and rooms, penetrating heavy rains, continuing dampness, and the severe winter of eastern Germany with its icy winds also made living there intolerable.

Despite the foregoing, the worst thing for me was the shortage of food. Without the Red Cross parcels supplementing the "short rations" provided by the Germans, many, if not most of us, would not have been able to survive. We tried a number of ways to make our meager food supply last each week. We found that we could eat well (a euphemistic term) for four days, but then the remaining three days, there would not be food to eat. That wasn't too good. Neither was eating every other day. Our final arrangement was to eat some food each day, stretching it out during the week. I went around being continually hungry and, along with others, fantasized about food, both verbally and in my thoughts. When captured, I was over six feet tall and weighed about 190 pounds, so these rations were meager. We shared the food equally. My past eating habits had not prepared me for this slow starvation.

Needing something to distract me from my many frustrations, all of which I could do nothing about, I became a Stalag Luft III "Commando." My activities involved acting as a lookout for German guards and "ferrets," who were German soldiers in blue fatigues. They carried long steel probes, hid under barracks, listened to conversations, looked for tunnels, and made themselves obnoxious. I also noticed who might get too close to where planning for controlled escapes and other activities were taking place. I assisted other POWs on forced marches and noticed who had difficulty in keeping up and might be shot if they lagged or were left behind. I was prepared at any time to participate in taking over the camp, overpowering the guards on a forced march, or aiding in mass controlled escape.

Early on in my meanderings around the West Compound, whose walkable perimeter was three-quarters of a mile long, I noticed that the RAF officers in the North Compound wore a black diamond-shaped piece of cloth on their left sleeve. This I learned was to commemorate 50 RAF airmen who were shot by the Gestapo, out of 76 who participated in a mass escape from that compound in late March of 1944. That was only about a month and a half before we took up residence in the West Compound. The reasons for the shootings, or why 50 of the 76 were shot, were not known. Three escapees, a Dutch airman and two Norwegians, had gotten away. The former reached England while the latter two made it to Sweden. The Germans returned the cremated ashes of the 50 murdered flyers to their comrades in the North Compound.

I also found that in our own barracks, there resided a United States naval air officer, Lt. Commander John Dunn, who was shot down and captured by the Germans on April 14, 1942, while a lieutenant junior grade. He held the distinction, if I am correct, of being the first American POW in Germany in World War II and the first American flyer to be confined In Stalag Luft III. (Note: I was commissioned a 2nd Lt. on July 15, 1943, spent exactly a year as a POW, and exited from the service on October 18, 1945 at the same 2nd Lt. rank. Granted that I was a civilian non-career type, but so what, didn't I and other POWs deserve a promotion?)

I knew that my time at Stalag Luft III was growing short when, in early January of 1945, I began to hear the muffled sounds of artillery coming from the east. As the days passed, the cannon sounds were getting louder, indicating movement toward the camp. It was, therefore, not surprising that the camp's staff put out the word on January 23, 1945, that everyone was expected to walk ten laps per day around the camp's perimeter. The total distance was seven and a half miles. It took about 15 minutes to complete one lap. Some of us had started this walking bit sometime earlier in order to maintain some degree of fitness. The new required regimen proved to be a hardship to many prisoners who were undernourished and out of condition, but it came in handy on our forthcoming march.

First Forced March, January 28, 1945. On Saturday, January 27, 1945, the word came about 9:00 p.m. to get ready to leave. There had been preparations for some time, including the making of packs and sleds. I later learned that the Russians were only 30 miles away when we left after 12:00 a.m. Sunday, January 28th. As we were sent single-file out of the camp, we were each tossed an unopened Red Cross food parcel. We formed columns of three and staggered forward into the ever-increasing fury of a blizzard. The column of ten thousand men extended for miles. We were kept moving for almost 48 hours before we were allowed to rest overnight. I was so cold at one point, when the line stopped, I knelt down to cut a heel of bread, resting it on my knee, and sawing at it with a knife, I didn't realize that I had cut through the bread until I saw blood dripping through my pants leg onto the snow.

Snow fell for four days in near zero temperatures, and ill-fitting packs, blisters, frozen feet and hands, and sickness all contributed to our misery. There were seemingly endless hours of marching with occasional rest periods and less frequent stops in barns along the way for much needed sleep. There were so many of us that at times groups took turns warming themselves while others waited in the blizzard for their turn at getting warmed up. I remember seeking shelter in an empty plant building with hundreds of others. The sounds and smells of myself and scores of others upchucking our guts, possibly because of drinking contaminated water, got to me in the worst way. I forced myself up and staggered out into the cold where the air was clean.

As a Commando, one of my assigned duties on the march was to assist stragglers. We didn't want to leave anyone behind to either freeze to death or be shot. It was somewhat strange to see prisoners helping guards by carrying their rifles. These guards were too old for combat duty and were not doing well under such adverse conditions. They drew the same rations as we kriegies. There were also tumbrel-like carts on which both prisoners and guards were being collected, those who could not keep going on foot.

Six days and 62 miles from Sagan (Stalag Luft III) we entrained at Spremberg for our next POW camp, this time at Nuremberg. At the start of this ride, we were given bread and margarine and a partial food parcel. Our transportation at this time was the French "forty and eight" freight cars. We were crammed, 50 men and a guard, into each car with barely enough room to sit down. The two-day trip, while better than our forced march in a blizzard, was still not good. I recall leaving this World War I type of transport thinking that now our conditions would improve. Little did I realize how wrong I would be.

Nuremberg, February 4, 1945. We arrived at Stalag VIII D, Nuremberg, on Sunday, February 4, 1945. Our camp at Sagan was a country club compared to what we found here. Conditions were deplorable. Italian prisoners had preceded us and when they left, the place was filthy. We were short of everything: food, heat, bedding, clothing, general sanitation, anti-vermin powders, and disinfectant. There was a shortage of cleaning materials, eating and cooking utensils, toilet facilities and toilet paper, drinking water, bathing facilities, exercise areas, and slit trenches. The list could go on and on. I estimate that my weight dropped an additional 20 pounds during my two-month stay here.

Our camp, I soon found out, was located within approximately two miles of a railroad checkpoint and marshalling yard. This area was continually subjected to both numerous daylight and night air raids, which kept us kriegies in a constant state of apprehension that the next bomb dropped close to us would be "it."

I resumed my Commando activities, although it was my under-standing that while we might have been able to physically take over this camp, we would be better off getting moved out. Our American officer, Colonel Darr H. Alkire, submitted a letter on February 28, 1945, to the Kommandant Stalag III stating the conditions that were felt to violate the July 27, 1929 Geneva Convention as regarding the treatment of POWs. This letter reads as follows:

Stalag Luft III
Nurnberg, Germany
28 February 1945

Subject: Complaints Respecting Conditions of Captivity.
To: The Kommandant Stalag Luft III

Under the provisions of the international convention relative to the treatment of prisoners of war published at Geneva Switz. July 27, 1929, of which the United States and the German Reich were signa-tory powers, The Senior American Officer of Stalag III presents in writing their basic requirements violated by the detaining power at this camp. Violations are as follows:

1. Proximity to Military Targets: Part III, Sect. III, Art. 9.
    Stalag Luft III is within approximately three kilometers of a rail-road choke point and marshalling yard. During the last two weeks the local area has been bombed by heavy aerial main efforts with an apparent attention to railroad targets. The dispersion of bombs both day and night has been close to this camp. There are no slit trenches or shelters which P.O.W.s are permitted to use during raids. Prisoners are kept in overcrowded huts at the point of guns. The location of the camp and local air raid precautionary policy is unjust and untenable and a protest of strongest nature is hereby registered for present and future consideration.

2. Inadequate Diet: Part III, Sect. II, Art. 11 and 12.
    The present German ration to P.O.W.s according to medical opin-
    ion is less than required for basic metabolism and inevitably will
    lead to loss of weight and starvation. Under the present unhy-
    gienic and unhealthy conditions resistance of men will become so
    lowered to render them rightly susceptible to any disease.

    A. German issue: Dehydrated vegetables are consistently
        wormy. No ersatz jam or honey has been issued. As closely
        as it can be figured the present rations total not more than
        1218 calories per man per day, which under even comfort-
        able circumstances is insufficient to sustain existence for
        an extended period. It is impossible even with an inflated
        imagination to consider the present German ration as a
        depot troop ration.

    B. Communal issue: Permission is required to distribute food
        from kitchen during air raids in order that such prepara-
        tions as are possible may be served warm.

    C. Clothing Repair and Replacement: There is no stack
        of clothing nor is there repair or replacement facilities
        provided as required by the detaining power. The major-
        ity of men from the Sagan area arrived here with only
        the clothing in which they stand. New purges from the
        Italian theatre are destitute. Clothing and shoes now being
        worn are rapidly wearing out. Overcoats and trousers are
        suggested.

3. Installations of Camp: Part LLL. Sect. II, Art. 10

    A. Overcrowding of Barracks: At the present time there are
        only 19 square feet of floor space per man and only 119
        cubic feet of air space. In this miniscule area our men
        must live, eat and sleep. This is a serious condition of
        overcrowding which may lead to respiratory borne epi-
        demics, such as cerebral spinal meningitis, pneumonia,
        influenza, etc. Aggravated by malnutrition and filth are as

present, conditions are apparently condoned by respon-
sible authorities.

B. Lack of Heat: No coal is provided for the barracks and
a shortage exists in the communal kitchens. The present ration is used in the hospital and seven kitchens. Two
kitchens have been closed and still only 180 kg. per kitchen
per day are available. A minimum of 400 kg. are requested.
This condition enhances unhealthfulness of the barracks,
dirtiness of food utensils and containers and means cold
or lukewarm food.

C. Shortage of Bedding: Many men do not have the depot
troop ration of blankets and many men have no beds of
any kind and must sleep on the cold damp floor. At present there are 1246 men sleeping on the floor. Stuffing
and palliases are vermin ridden with no replacements,
no opportunity to clean those in use. It is felt that no
depot troops of the detaining power are subject to this
treatment.

D. Poor Lighting: Lighting of the barracks and aborts is below standard for depot troops and no convenience of
accessibility to abort is afforded between the hours of
2300 and 0600 hours. No intelligent method of commu-
nication with the hospital or for emergency is afforded
during lockup hours, other than by voice from block to
block. A light warning system of some type is an immediate necessity. Night aborts having no lights contribute to
more filthiness.

4. Hygiene in Camp: Part III, Sect. II, Chapter 3, Art. 3.
A. Inadequate washing and bathing facilities. It has been
planned but not put into effect to give showers to P.O.W.s
once each two weeks. The shower officers report that the
Abwher Dept. has interfered unnecessarily and a better
understanding is necessary in order to utilize what few

facilities are available. No laundry facilities, the lack of hot water, soap, and space necessary for washing and drying clothing, dishes and food containers lead to infection and dysentery. Wash houses have not more than two cold water faucets and due to prevalent overcrowding means 450 men must depend on two cold water outlets.

B. Vermin: Rats, mice, lice, bed bugs and fleas are prevalent throughout the camp. Anti-vermin powders and disinfectant are not available. Delousing programs are too sporadic to be effective. The present disinfectant is so weak that it will not destroy vermin eggs and doubtful that it even liquidates the living organism. Indicative of the filthy conditions, a blow torch is necessary for the elimination of eggs and larva.

C. No Cleaning Material: For cleaning of barracks, kitchens, aborts, clothing and person of P.O.W.s is not available. Brushes, brooms and mops are nonexistent. Disinfectant and anti-vermin powder is not issued. 50 rolls for over five thousand men has been issued in the way of toilet paper.

D. Lack of Eating and Cooking Utensils: Very few utensils for eating and cooking have been issued and most prisoners eat from a can.

E. Shortage of Medical Supplies: It is practically impossible to obtain any medical supplies from German sources. Emergency supplies from the move to Nurnberg from Sagan are depleted and there appears to be no possibility of replacement.

F. General Sanitation, Debris and Garbage Disposal: Night abort cans leak and containers are not furnished in sufficient numbers. Urinals in some aborts are leaking badly. Aborts are open and will be a potential source of epidemics during the fly season. No storage space is available in barracks for keeping clothing and food in sanitary conditions. Few tools for general repairs and improvements have been issued and the few tools made locally have been confiscated by Abwher representatives. Windows in barracks are in bad need of repair.

5. Mail and Personal Parcel Censorship: Part III, Sect. IV Art. 36, 37, 40.
Mail has been at this camp more than a week without being distributed. Distribution of parcels policy is in need of classification.

6. Religious Activities: Part III, Sect. II, Chap. 4, Art. 16.
Protected personnel. Access to all compounds and permission for access to outside hospitals have been most unsatisfactory for both Protestant and Catholic chaplains. The presence of a guard is not only unnecessary but also seems to imply a disregard for the chaplain's office. Parole walks should be separate for protected personnel and thereby not prejudiced to other P.O.W.s.

7. Entertainment and Recreation: Part III, Sect. II, Chap. 4, Art. 17.
Books are practically nonexistent and congestion of billeting in camp necessitates utilization of space normally used as a theatre and chapel for barracks. Intellectual and spiritual welfare is suffering under insurmountable obstacles.

Recreation. Ground space for calisthenics or organized athletics is not available. This total lack of facilities adds to the mental and physical discontent of all concerned.

8. Canteen Supplies: Part III, Sect II, Chap. 2, Art. 12.
Canteen inoperative. No provisions are being made for purchase of local articles. Razors, blades, soap, tooth powder, brushes, combs, watches, barber supplies and mirrors are badly needed.

Authorities of the detaining power having announced their helplessness in alleviating the present deplorable circumstances due to transportation and material shortages. The S.A.O. suggests the following course of action subject to the approval of the German Reich, the United States and the protecting power.

    A. Parole March and Internment: P.O.W.s of this camp will undertake, under parole not to escape, a march of not more than 20 kms. per day to the Swiss border, where they will be interned for the duration of the war with Germany. Food could be provided according to the German march rations or one Red Cross parcel per man per 75 kms.

    B. Parole March to New Location: P.O.W.s of this camp will undertake, under parole not to escape, a march of 20 kms. per day to any new location out of the military target area more accessible to Red Cross supplies of food, clothing and medical supplies. Given proper tools and materials they will do what construction work is necessary. Food supplies will be in accordance with "A" above.

It is requested that a representative of the protecting power be permitted to visit this camp and confirm the veracity of these statements.

(signed) Darr H. Alkire
Col., US Army
Senior American Officer.*

    * This document has been reproduced exactly from the original.

    On the day when we moved out on our second forced march, the senior American officer (SAO) was concerned that no unauthorized personnel remained in camp. The reason was that they would be killed by the Germans in their search when we were all supposed to have left. I, along with the other American Commandos, was going through the barracks making sure that they were empty. On passing the SAOs administrative office on my way out of the camp, I saw a copy of the above letter to the Kommandant, Stalag Luft III, posted on the bulletin board and added it to my collection of memorabilia.

Second Forced March, April 4, 1945. The senior American officer, Col. Alkire, was in charge of the organization and control of this forced march. The German commander had agreed to this and to a march of no longer than 20 kilometers (about 12 miles) per day in return for the SAO preserving order.

I walked out of the camp with some ten thousand others, three abreast. Each of us was given a Red Cross food parcel. This march took us ten days, with our destination being, as we soon learned, Stalag VII, Moosberg, located in southern Germany, not far from Munich.

This march again produced stiff limbs, blisters, and tired bodies. We walked through heavily wooded regions that were made dangerous by almost complete darkness and heavy rain. The latter added pounds to our packs and soaked us to the skin. Much of the trip was spent traversing hilly country. Our main danger was being strafed by our own planes. All around us we could see groups of bombers, bombing targets, and swarms of our fighters circling about. These fighters appeared many times as if they were going to strafe us. Fortunately, we were able to lay out POW signs on the ground, made out of odds and ends of white material, to signal them. A white arrow pointed in the direction of the march.

I became quite adept at scrounging kohlrabi, a cabbage-like vegetable, and potatoes from the countryside, both of which were eaten raw. I remember one night's foray into the loft of a farmer's barn. After locating his seed potatoes (the best were not too good to liberate), the flooring broke with a loud crash, dropping me on top of the desired potatoes. I scampered out of there as fast as I could and was very frightened since I had placed myself in harm's way.

There were two disturbing reports that I heard while walking to Moosberg. One was about the death of President Franklin Roosevelt. The local citizenry, with great delight and satisfaction, yelled this news at us as we passed by. The other report was in the form of a rumor, which I and many others heard repeated many times, that Hitler had given the word to kill all of us rather than let us be liberated. In this way, we would no longer present a threat to the Third Reich by returning to fight against Germany. Fortunately, nothing came of this last rumor.

Stalag VII A, Moosberg, April 14, 1945. This camp, according to rumor, held an estimated 115,000 prisoners representing many nationalities and speaking 15 different languages. It was literally a series of closely connected wire enclosures. It became known as the "United Nations of Prisoners" as various camps that were not liberated were evacuated south toward Munich. I lived in a tent that housed approximately three hundred men. We were packed together in three parallel lines with just enough room to turn over without disturbing our neighbors. A layer of wood shavings on the floor served as our mattress. These tents were neither heated, lighted, or properly ventilated.

As the days passed and the war came closer to us, the wire barriers separating the individual compounds were torn down by the prisoners. No interference was made by the guards except that until the day we were liberated, the Russian prisoners in the most central compound continued to be segregated from the rest of us.

LIBERATION, April 29, 1945, a Sunday. The sound of artillery was plainly heard close by; then bullets began to whistle through our camp. I spent several hours lying as flat on the ground as I could. When things got quiet and I heard the sound of tanks creeping toward the camp, I made my way to the front gates. General George Patton came up to the camp in a tank leading the 14th Armored Division attached to his Third Army. He was all aglitter with his general's bars gleaming on his helmet and clothing, pearl-handled guns, and looking neat and military-like. We, on the other hand, looked ragged, disreputable, and dirty. I heard the general say that he was glad we enlisted men had held up as well as we did. A number of us responded that we were officers. It was not until many years later when I saw the motion picture *Patton*, starring George C. Scott, that I fully understood why the general referred to us as enlisted men. It was because we didn't fit his concept that an officer should look like a military man at all times:

i.e., clean, neat, and trim, erect and alert under all conditions. We just didn't fit his bill of particulars at this time.

The sight of the German flag coming down and "Old Glory" being raised brought many a tear to our eyes... Now, we could go home!

With best regards,
Norman H. Roth

20

RETURN TO HOLLAND

Forty-five years later, on the day I returned to Holland, the Resistance leader Marinus de Bruin's wife, Kina, had died. Betty and I attended her wake and five days later we attended the church funeral. She was buried in a plain wooden box and was attended by pallbearers dressed in formal wear and top hats.

While in Holland, we visited Flevoland, a polder, a land below sea level that was reclaimed from the Ijsselmeer (formerly the Zuider Zee) by building dykes and pumping the water out. From the fifteenth century they built dykes at the North Sea and pumped water out with windmills. They built slopes to catch the water that was drained, and kept the saltwater out and brought fresh water from the rivers.

Towns with populations of 40 to 50 thousand exist there, all of them 20 to 30 feet below sea level.

They have found ships and downed planes from World War II while building and dredging in the sea. They are still developing land that is owned by the government and rented or leased or sold by the government. This reclaimed land would be infertile because of the salt content and would take about seven years to neutralize. Many gardens and farms looked like they were one hundred years old or more. All were surrounded by 45-foot dykes.

Land is so scarce that it is hardly ever sold. It is handed down to the next generation in the family. This land reclamation is actually a centuries-old process that dates back to the 1400s and is still basically done the same way. The citizenry want to keep the government from reclaiming some of the shoreline because they want to preserve the hunting and fishing along the waterways. Several large cities, many smaller villages, and numerous farms have been developed there since World War II.

Each day of our visit to Holland in 1988, the de Bruin family would have something scheduled for us to do. A ride on the Rhine River in a tourist boat was very interesting. We embarked at Westerbouwing and debarked in Arnhem and went back by bus to Westerbouwing to the car. One morning Aaltij, Betty, and I went to Arie's weekend camp in a nature reserve in the Springendal area, about one kilometer from the German border. Rijk, Arie's wife, served us coffee and cookies. Their camp was very beautiful. From there, Arie, Aaltij, Betty, and I went by car to a castle at Singraven that was built in 1448. We visited an old watermill that is still used to grind grain into flour. We then motored to Bensheim, Germany, and visited another castle on a hill, built in 1160. From there we went to Gronau, Germany, and did some shopping. Arie can speak German because he worked along the German border as a tax collector. He served as our interpreter. We returned via Enschede, Hengelo, and Oldenzaal to Arie's camp. I remembered the trips I had made around the countryside many years ago.

Rijk gave Betty two handmade necklaces. Aaltij sent souvenir spoons home with Betty for our children. They were all very gracious ladies. We returned to Bill and Toos de Bruin's home in time for supper. We also visited the quaint town of Staphorst, where they still wear wooden shoes and traditional costumes. Next we visited three war cemeteries: the cemetery at Grebbeberg, where several hundred soldiers died in defense of Holland against the Nazi invasion in May, 1940; the Canadian War Cemetery in Holten, where Canadian and Polish soldiers are buried; the British Cemetery in Arnhem-Oosterbeek. We also saw a memorial to the Resistance Force members who were shot by the Nazis. Two of them I knew, Klaus Huibers and Gebrit Salomons.

Another interesting place was called Geithoorn, "The Venice of Holland." There were no roads and the residents traveled by boat. There are still about three hundred windmills in operation, pumping water and grinding grain. The country is small but very beautiful. No litter anywhere. The people treated us like royalty. We received many gifts. Most citizens are very industrious and extremely clean. The homes are beautiful and every yard is manicured to perfection, with beautiful flowers and gardens. If you admire their belongings they will try to give them to you. The Jan Amsink family gave us a beautiful Delft plate.

It was a very emotional time and it was so good to see all of the wonderful people who fed and took care of me and many others. We servicemen who were helped owe our lives to them.

Those who we saw on our trip were:

Marinus de Bruin

Willem (Bill) and Toos de Bruin

Arie and Rijk de Bruin

Aaltij (de Bruin) and Jan Ligtenberg

Fay de Bruin and Hendrick Hekman

Marie de Bruin

A. Jan Kolkman

J.H. Kamphuis

Baron Van Pallandt's daughter of Ommen,
Mrs. Adrie de La Porte

Nete Salomons, the widow of Gebrit Salomons
of Hardenberg

THE PLAYBOY CREW 1943-1944

Amsink family's five surviving children from Ane, Gramsbergen: Gerrit, Hendrikje, Yennigje, Hendrick, and Jan

Willem and Clary (Smeenck) Jonkind, of Almelo

P.C. (Piet) Meijer of Den Ham, a member of the Dutch Research Association for Crashed Allied Aircraft

Bill and I called Greta (Smeenck) Tenny in Florida, and we visited for a few minutes.

When I began to tell these stories around the campfire in Arizona about the Dutch people helping the Allied flyers, I was asked by some, "Why did they risk so much?" Their whole families and homes could have been destroyed by the Germans in the flash of a firing squad bullet.

The answer came to me when I reflected during the nights around the campfires. I was telling the stories to a young man, Jason, from a generation who had never heard a first-person account about World War II. I could remember the same expressions in the eyes of the children in Holland during the war. We were the sons, brothers, husbands, and fathers, all fighting for freedom for our families in America.

The Dutch families were also fighting in their way, aiding Allied fighters through the Resistance Force the best way they knew how and for the very same reason...Freedom!

I felt honored when my father asked me to assist him in revising and republishing his memoir. It has been a labor of love. I have enjoyed this process greatly.

To me, the most important word in this book is the final word of Chapter 20, "Freedom." It is our most valued right. It is because of these brave men of the *Playboy* crew and countless other men and women who have defended America that we have our freedom. I would like to thank each and every one of them. It is we who now stand on the shoulders of these patriots.

Brian Alan Pipes

LaVergne, TN USA
09 June 2010
185519LV00005B/201/P

9 781432 758493